First Ladies OWN YOUR DAY!

Rachel D. Blake

Largo, MD

ISBN 9781562295219

Christian Living Books, Inc.
P.O. Box 7584
Largo, MD 20792
christianlivingbooks.com
We bring your dreams to fruition.

Dedication

I dedicate this book to my three daughters Rachel, Ron-esha, Rae-Ocean Blake and my three sisters Ruth Esther, who went to be with the Lord on March 6, 2020, Ira Ali, and Deborah Sulier.

CONTENTS

INTRODUCTION

I am a third-generation Church of God in Christ member. My father was a district superintendent, and my mother was a district missionary, which makes me a pastor's kid. I am the seventh of eight children from California. I've been married to my one and only husband for 31 years. He is also a pastor's kid and a second-generation Church of God in Christ member. He is the ninth of twelve children from Birmingham, Alabama. In 2008, we followed the instructions of God and began our ministry.

In 2013, I accepted the invitation to be a district missionary and my husband became a district superintendent in 2018. We have been blessed with three daughters. The oldest is in medical school at Howard University. Our second daughter is completing her studies at U.C. Berkeley with the goal of pursuing medicine as well. Our youngest is a junior at Metro State University in Colorado. She will also pursue studies in the science discipline.

I was inspired to write this book for several reasons. One night, I was scrolling through my phone and came across an article that said 76% of first ladies within the church are depressed. I could not believe what I was reading; it almost left me breathless. I shared this information with my husband and insisted the statistics could not be correct. How is that possible? Why are so many first ladies depressed?

It was then that I said to my husband I must talk to the first ladies. I have to reach out to them and let them know exactly who they are because depression is not an option. Depression is a foul spirit from the pit of hell that is often deeply rooted in a dysfunctional relationship with God.

The Enemy's strategy is to afflict our minds; however, we must remember what to focus on to keep it sound:

> Finally, brothers and sisters, whatever is true, whatever is noble, whatever is right, whatever is pure, whatever is lovely, whatever is admirable—if anything is excellent or praiseworthy—think about such things.
> (Philippians 4:8 NIV)

We have too many good things to think about to let the Enemy bombard our minds with lies. God will keep every first lady in perfect peace if she focuses her attention on Him because she trusts Him (Isaiah 26:3). God Himself goes before us and will never leave or forsake us, so we must not be afraid or discouraged (Deuteronomy 31:8).

Realizing the magnitude of pain other first ladies endure and, which seemingly goes unnoticed, alarmed me. Since 2008, I had been praying to God about the uncertainty that comes with being a first lady. Reading this article caused me to go to God in prayer; I was commissioned to help first ladies. In my quiet time, God revealed my direction. It became clear that all the pitfalls and blessings I traversed on my journey to being a first lady would finally serve a purpose. God said it was time to write a book. And I did.

I have written this book for every first lady around the world, in every denomination, and of every nationality. Being a first lady is a ministry. God has chosen us because He knows with all that is within us, we will do what we are called to do. When God took a rib from Adam's side to create Eve, it was representative of our roles as helpmates to our husbands as we journey through life according to God's blueprint.

Even with all our hero qualities, first ladies are humans also. We hear, feel, hurt, enjoy, achieve, and rise to the occasion just as others do. Both God and our husbands can trust us to overcome every obstacle that comes our way. With prayer and supplication, we will face them head-on. When the righteous cry out, the Lord hears them and delivers them from all their troubles. The Lord is close to the brokenhearted and saves those who are crushed in spirit (Psalm 34:17-18). God wants us to work alongside our husbands in the ministries He has given us and our ministries will be heard! They will grow into the loving gardens of roses, orchids, lilies, baby's breath, tulips, and all the other beautiful flowers God designed them to be.

I also wrote this book to say to all first ladies you are very special. You said yes to your husbands when they said yes to God. You did it even though you had no idea what being a first lady entailed. This book is for all first ladies because you are smart and observant. You are smart enough to know you can do all things through Christ who strengthens you. And you are observant enough to know when the Enemy comes in like a flood, the Spirit of the Lord shall lift a standard against him (Isaiah 59:19).

I want to remind each of you that you are truly intelligent and wise. Proverbs 14:1 says every wise woman builds her house, but every foolish woman tears her house down with her own hands. We are intelligent enough to recognize we are first in our husbands' lives after God. The church is God's house; therefore, we will not do anything foolish or let any foolish person destroy it. We will not partake in any foolishness in or out of God's house.

Another objective of this book is to let all first ladies know you are beautifully and wonderfully made regardless of your size, height, or age (Psalm 139:14). Walk with confidence and humility knowing on any given day, whatever the Enemy throws your way, you are covered by God. We are more than conquerors through Him who loves us.

> No, in all these things we are more than conquerors through him who loved us. (Romans 8:37 NIV)

I desire to tell all present and future first ladies although we have never met, you are loved. I want to personally tell you I love you. Regardless of what you have been through or what you will encounter, you will never be alone.

First ladies throughout this entire world share the same feelings of loneliness. They have the same questions you have. They cry the way you cry. We can identify with one another; therefore, we need each other. We have a connection, not only through Christ but by being our husbands' number one fans, their smallest critics, and biggest cheerleaders.

Instead of viewing each other through the same perspective as outsiders, let's look at each other through the eyes God has given to first ladies: eyes of love, compassion, inspiration, forgiveness, and trustworthiness. We should see one another for who we are and who we will become in Christ, not for who people say we are and think we should be. When we change our views, we will see what we are doing in Christ truthfully, not through the false accusations of people. By the way, this is how God molds and shapes first ladies.

PART I

How Did I Get Here?

Chapter 1

WHAT IN THE WORLD WAS I THINKING?

God, how did I get here?" I asked God this question many times and got the same answer: "From a young girl you always said you wanted to be a pastor's wife, and I made it happen."

What in the world was I thinking? Where did this idea stem from? For as long as I can remember, I was in love with being a pastor's wife. Growing up, the only thing my younger sister and I did other than go to church was play church. While our friends were playing house and dolls, we were playing church. We were so committed we would go to church, come home, and play church. We would go to school, come home, and play church. We would go to visit relatives, come home, and play church. We would go to my best friend's house who was also a pastor's kid and play church. Then, once we arrived home, we would resume our favorite pastime–playing church. At each church service we had, despite who else wanted to, I would always give the message. I looked forward to playing church not so I could assume the position as pastor, but so I could teach the Word of God. I even recall anointing our dolls' foreheads with cooking oil from the kitchen; it was my job to make sure all our members were saved.

One day, I asked my mother if she enjoyed being a pastor's wife. When she was finished talking to me, I was filled with joy and excitement by her response. She told me being a pastor's wife entailed helping and praying for people. Often, when people called the house for the pastor to pray for them and he wasn't there, she would step in and pray for them in his absence. She expressed how being a pastor's wife gave her an opportunity to listen to the cries of women, hear their problems, and share scriptures or wisdom God revealed to guide and comfort them. She told stories about how she would support them by accompanying them to their doctors' appointments or grocery shopping.

As she spoke to me, not once did she utter anything negative, which made me more than ready to be a pastor's wife; thank you, Mom. But she left out one thing: being a pastor's wife is a ministry. I can't say for certain if she knew this or not...perhaps she did and didn't want to pressure me by using the word "ministry." It sounds heavy as if it entails loads of work; honestly, it does sometimes. At the time, I was very young, and I know the last thing she wanted to do was discourage me.

Infectious Excitement

Mom spoke so highly of the role. The excitement in her voice and her body language as she explained what pastors' wives did were infectious. She said their responsibility is also to help build the church, visit the sick, and participate in outreach programs. She also told me playing the piano, singing to the Lord, telling the church about God's goodness, and sharing the love of God by witnessing beyond the church walls to strangers are

My mother, District Missionary Lucille Howard

activities first ladies should be involved in. Everyone may not make it into the house of God; therefore, we must go out into the highways and hedges, and compel them to come in that God's house may be filled (Luke 14:23). She said as first ladies, our lives should be the mirror that reflects the image of Christ (2 Corinthians 3:18). My mother spoke with such compassion, excitement, and energy that all I could do was look forward with great anticipation to my future as a pastor's wife.

As the years went by, I had the same conversation with my aunt, asking her how she liked being a first lady. It was strange how identical her response was to my mother's. She shared the same energy, excitement, and passion my mother had as she expressed her love for being a pastor's wife. Looking back, I don't know if they had discussed this beforehand with each other or if that was a corporate response they gave to anyone inquiring about being a first lady. Perhaps they wanted to inspire and nothing else, but I oftentimes wonder if it was a plot to recruit me. Nevertheless, speaking with both of them solidified my desire to be a pastor's wife.

Since then, I have posed this same question to many pastors' wives and their answers were quite the opposite. Each response was heavy with negative words and an uninspired outlook. Unfortunately, of all the first ladies I've ever asked, my mother and aunt were the only two who were encouraged about being a pastor's wife.

When I first met my husband, he told me his ultimate goal in life was to preach the gospel. I expressed to him our desires aligned as I wanted to be a pastor's wife. At that moment, we knew God had ordained our union. Although our ministry has and is still being tested, we are determined to continue to persevere until God says, "Well done, thou good and faithful servant." With each trial and triumph, I must admit that sometimes in reflection I ask myself, "How did I get here?"

No Worries

Now ladies, this next sentence might take you for a spin, but listen closely because I firmly stand behind every word. I have never in my life worried about the age I would be when I got married or was concerned with if God had forgotten to give me a husband. I'm pretty sure most women have heard countless times that our biological clocks are ticking. We are also too familiar with the idea that we must look for a husband. I've witnessed the detrimental nature of this flawed ideology. Young women place a time limit on their love lives and older women pressure them to find husbands. I have seen countless ladies buying into this same mindset. But I praise God so much that I've never lost sleep over the idea of a husband.

God has always given me the heart and mind to pursue Him and not a man. I knew in due time, when God was ready to bless me with a husband, I wouldn't have to search. My husband would find me.

> He who finds a wife finds a good thing, and these things obtaineth favor of the Lord. (Proverbs 18:22 NKJV)

My husband and I first locked eyes when he came to my church during a Christmas revival; he found me praising and worshiping God. A week later, my sister Ira introduced us after our church convention, and the rest is history.

I never lost sleep over the idea of a husband.

Three years after marriage, God gave us His blessing to relocate to Denver, Colorado. Fast forward 16 years and three daughters later, I received devastating news from my husband. He explained to me how reenlisting in the Navy would further his career. No later than the ink had dried on the paper, they decided to deploy him to Afghanistan–a hotspot warzone at the time. I can't begin to describe the blow my daughters and I felt. It was as if we could literally see our covering leaving. He was scheduled to be there for one year, but praise God, he returned home safely after five months.

"It Is Time"

One of the first conversations we had was my husband telling me God said it is time to start our ministry. I asked him if he was sure; to which he replied, "Yes, I am." I said to the Lord, "My mother didn't mention our startup church would consist of just our children as the members or that it would be held in our house instead of a church building."

Months later, after receiving our pastor's blessings, my husband openly announced to our home church that God had instructed him to pastor his own church. My husband had been the assistant pastor for two years. You would never have known he held this position by the way we were treated and addressed. Only one person in the entire church would even acknowledge us as the assistant pastor and wife.

Now, let me give you the full picture. There was a time my husband and I attended our annual church banquet. Our pastor and first lady were seated at the head table. My husband and I, as assistant pastor and wife, sat to the right of them–and rightfully so. However, it was a shock to us and the congregation to see another couple seated to the left of our pastor. It appeared as if two preachers were vying for the same position. This particular preacher was given a church by our pastor, lost it, and returned. In spite of that, he was being promoted while other faithful elders and wives who had never left the church were being sidelined. You could imagine the numerous murmurs of the saints this act sparked; the calls I received were endless. We saw it brewing in our faces, but we continued to hold our peace and trust God. The following year, this particular preacher began pastoring the church.

The last Sunday at our former church while my husband was preaching his final sermon, our senior pastor and about fifteen other church leaders did the unthinkable. Instead of staying in the sanctuary to enjoy the message for the last time, they were in our church kitchen eating dinner. To add insult to injury, had my family and I not gone into the church's kitchen after service to say goodbye, they just wouldn't have bid us farewell. I guess when it is time to eat, the stomach is king.

As a man and woman of God, you don't expect to be mistreated by leaders in your own church. We gave more than 100% of ourselves and our finances to our former church even though God only requires us to give ten percent of our earnings to Him and a freewill offering. You may be thinking it's our fault for giving more than what was required of us but we were always taught you cannot lead from behind.

> A tenth of the produce of the land, whether grain or fruit, is the Lord's, and is holy. (Leviticus 27:30 TLB)

> Honor the Lord with your wealth, with the first fruits of all your crops. (Proverbs 3:9 NIV)

These verses are essentially saying to give a portion, specifically a tenth of whatever you make back to God. First fruits are a biblical way of giving thanks to God before you do anything else with your finances. You should feel honored knowing you are respecting God's Word, which is your reasonable service. This applies to your tithing and yourself.

Ladies, I mentioned this because if you are thinking about joining the ministry for financial gain, you need to look for another profession. You will not receive a great deal of money for being a first lady. Actually, money should never be the reason you become a pastor's wife. We don't work for the gospel; the gospel works for us when we use the gifts God has given to us. As we continue to operate in spiritual leadership, in due time, God will let those who we preside over consider us worthy of double honor, especially those who labor in preaching and teaching.

Scripture says you shall not muzzle an ox when it treads out the grain and the laborer deserves his wages (1 Timothy 5:18).

In due time, you will be rewarded.

When my husband and I began our ministry, we refused to take any offerings from our congregation. We only did so seven years after our ministry began, choosing to meet the needs of the members first as we built God's kingdom. First ladies, do not be disheartened if you are not receiving a Women's Day or 5th Sunday offering. Continue to operate in your God-ordained ministry and in due time, you will be rewarded.

> And in the same house remain, eating and drinking such things as they give: for the laborer is worthy of his hire. Go not from house to house. (Luke 10:7)

Stealing Members

My husband made it clear to our former church that he wouldn't take any members with him. When he uttered those words, I thought to myself, "Are you crazy?!" and I am sure my facial expression showed this. At that moment, I had so many questions for God. "Is my husband slow? Why doesn't he understand he is starting his own church? Does he know we don't have any members?" A part of me felt leaders should never discourage anyone from helping build God's kingdom. I knew this and so did our three daughters.

On our way home from the church that Sunday, our girls asked me why their dad announced he did not want the church members to join us. We had been faithful members ever since they had been in this world. To them, it did not make sense; we had so many friends there.

"Why wouldn't Dad want them to follow us?" As usual, they looked to Mom for answers and clarity. This was the wrong time to ask me this question as I was still angry, but they were waiting for a response. I had to explain to them their dad didn't believe in stealing members from other churches–neither did I. I said we believed in making it known God ordered us to start a new ministry. If He leads anyone to join in spreading the gospel then that is fine. If He doesn't, so be it.

I Had a Few Questions

My husband became a pastor but only half of me was happy; the other half wasn't. The more I prayed about this situation, the more I realized it wasn't that half of me didn't want my husband to be a pastor; I just didn't agree with the way he handled the situation, neither did our daughters. I think sometimes as leaders, we try so hard not to step on anyone's toes when God is saying, "All I need you to do is accept My will with all of your heart. I will send who I want to fellowship with you."

I am learning that we don't get to decide who we want to be a part of our church family; God does. We have to let God's will be done, especially when it comes to who fellowships with us. I can't speak for other first ladies but when I first became a pastor's wife, I was expecting our church to grow each and every week. Notice I said pastor's wife, instead of saying first lady. This is because, before the year 2000, we didn't address pastors' wives as first ladies. We always called them pastors' wives. Perhaps this is because we weren't into titles as much as we are now, but there's absolutely nothing wrong with this.

I was expecting our church to grow each week.

I was expecting our church to take off non-stop. I personally couldn't see a reason why it shouldn't have. First of all, my husband always wanted to preach the gospel more than anything else in his life. Second,

God has gifted him to teach the Word of God under the anointing better than anyone else on this side of heaven–after my father. Now that Superintendent Howard is with our heavenly Father, my husband has moved to number 1. Third, I have always wanted to be a pastor's wife. Fourth, my husband and I were living for the Lord with every moving part of our minds, bodies, souls, and spirits.

We also abided by Proverbs 22:6 by training up our girls in the way they should go so that when they are old, they will not depart from it. And honey, it certainly wasn't our finances. So, there was no earthly reason why we should have started a church in our home and watched it grow in slow motion. I had a few questions for my husband. Since you knew it was the time to start a church, did you let people know? Were you spreading the news and inviting people to visit or were you just totally relying on God to do all this for you?

My father, District Superintendent Norris Howard

Chapter 2

A WONDERFUL AND BLESSED LIFE?

Although I was too young to recall how my father began our first church in Bakersfield, I am very familiar with our second church, which was in Berkeley. My father was from the old school and very strict in his beliefs, but we had tremendous respect for him. Though he could have purchased a church building, my father instead concluded that since my older sisters and brothers did not want to live for God, they were at least going to live in God's house... and we really lived in the church. I don't mean we were at church so often and long that it seemed as if we lived there. No, I'm speaking literally. The restroom the church members used throughout service was the bathroom we used every morning to get ready. The nice church seat the pastor and elders sat on was really our roller bed. As soon as church was over and all of the saints left, my brothers would let the seat out; my older sisters would cover our sleeper seat with the sheets, and we would lie down and go to sleep.

I would always complain to my parents that they were the reason I did not tell the truth. I had a big family so everyone in the neighborhood knew us. You know how word travels; everyone knew we lived in a church. Even my closest friends had the nerve to ask me if I really lived in a church, and you know what I told them, right? I had my answer ready, which was an elaborate tale about architecture and how our church was completely separated from our house. I couldn't tell the truth; can you blame me? It was a little embarrassing. Honestly, our friends would've accepted us regardless, but it was a problem for my mom and her children.

I will never forget how my father would pray over us every time we had church service. He would begin by praying for my oldest brother and then go down the line according to our ages. I was the seventh of eight children. When he got to my name, he would always skip me and pray for my youngest sister. Then he would circle back to pray for me and when I say he took his time, I mean it. It made me very uncomfortable. I could not understand why he spent so much time praying for me. I wasn't an out-of-hand child, but he prayed so long and hard, as if somehow God would stop me from "sinning."

I had six older sisters and brothers who were awful. At that point, they did not attend church anymore and one of them was a drug dealer in the Bay Area. All I wanted to do was wear pants and secure a spot on Soul Train. See my problem? I felt my father had the members of the church thinking I was some big-time sinner. As an adult, I finally got the courage to ask him why he would pray so long for me. He said he did it because the ministry God had for me would be different from that of my siblings. What a revelation! But as a child, that did not make me feel any better. When I became a first lady his prayers for me finally changed–they got even longer!

Constant Drama

As the pastor's wife, my mother had so much to endure. I mentioned earlier our family was big, right? The way our home-church was set up, we lived in a big duplex. We lived downstairs in our church while my mother's sister and her nine children lived upstairs. My aunt was a backslider, so other than her youngest daughter, she and her household never attended church. Just imagine every weekend there was always either a big party, fighting, or accidents going on upstairs.

Picture Sunday morning service being interrupted by the sound of gunshots. On this particular Sunday, we ran out of church only to see the horrific incident of my brother being shot by his wife. The bullet missed his heart by 1/4th of an inch. In the midst of the constant drama, was a little section of the house my mother called her own. It was on the opposite end of the church and she had it fixed up as her living room. I can honestly say this was my favorite part of the entire complex other than the kitchen. It felt like a real home.

With such a big family, we were blessed to have four bedrooms and two bathrooms downstairs. Unfortunately, at least once a week, my aunt who lived upstairs would run her shower, and water would leak through our ceiling. I remember seeing the tears in my mother's eyes every time this happened. She couldn't do normal first lady things like host brunches with the other pastors' wives.

My mother did everything from cooking and selling dinners on the weekend to personally chauffeuring members to and from Sunday service. She worked as a first lady up until her death, even after she and my father had separated. My mother never wanted our church to fall short of its kingdom obligations as a result of her personal relationship with my father. This was not the dream she envisioned. Many days and nights, her eyes would be filled with tears due to circumstances, but the humble, quiet, holy woman of God she was kept her from openly complaining. My mother loved being a first lady because we were all there together as a family but over time, she became ashamed and unhappy. The circumstances prevented her from truly enjoying her home.

Husband–Father–Pastor

My father wore many hats. Not only was he the oldest adjutant of the Church of God in Christ when he passed away, but he was also a well-respected foreman by trade, a member of the union, and a degree holder. Don't get it twisted; my father was the best dad a family could want and I was certainly a daddy's girl. However, from what my mother would say and my sisters and brothers saw, he was not the husband or pastor God had called him to be.

My father was very educated in the Word of God. He graduated with honors in theology at Shiloh Christian College in northern California. I share this so you can better grasp the situations my mother encountered as a first lady; maybe some of you first ladies can relate. My older sisters shared with me stories of how my father would say hurtful words about my mother in front of the congregation. He would preach about her appearance, how she did not have big legs and ridiculed her small frame. He would even go overboard expressing how she wore the biggest, prettiest hats in the church, but didn't have long hair down her back. This happened countless Sundays. I asked my mom why she didn't gracefully stick her foot out to trip him when he walked by to shake the saint's hands after church service. Even better, why didn't she tell him off on the way home? She said they often drove in separate cars, but one Sunday when she was fed up, she let him have it at home. She just put one hand on her hip and used the other to point at him while saying, "You need to preach the gospel and not me!" Let's just say that's one message he didn't recycle.

She worked as a first lady up until her death.

"Mom, how could you put up with his actions?" I asked.

She would simply say, "He didn't know any better." She believed he did not know a real man of God wouldn't treat his wife this way. In her mind, his real calling was to remain an assistant pastor, not to pastor. Despite my parent's personal relationship, my mother instilled in my siblings and me to always love and respect him as our father and a man of God.

> Touch not mine anointed, and do my prophets no harm.
> (1 Chronicles 16:22)

Of course, witnessing all this made me question the veracity of my mother's wonderful and blessed life as a pastor's wife. How could she subject herself to mistreatment? She would look at me with a smile and say, "Being a pastor's wife is a position chosen by God." In her eyes, it is a sacred position that takes a very special lady to fill and when God puts you in this position, you take it very seriously. She believed when people mistreat first ladies, we should never take it out on God. Rather, we should give unto God everything He requires of us in love; that's why He only chooses a few women for this position. Romans 8:30 reminds us that the few He chooses, He qualifies.

Chapter 3

WHEN I BECAME MY MOTHER

I wonder how many first ladies actually knew what to expect when they first stepped into that position. Did any of you ask: "What am I doing here? Where is the book to warn me about all that will come at me? Where are the guidelines to remind me of the goodness of being a first lady? When does the joy kick in? I love God and my husband, but I can't quite navigate all that is being thrown at me right now. Where are the encouraging words from the saints?"

I presented these questions to God in 2008 when I began my journey as a first lady with no idea when or how He would respond. Then, one day He answered me very clearly and said, "Being a first lady is a ministry that comes from the Most High, King of kings, and Lord of lords." Hearing God speak those words to me filled me with the same joy and strength I had when I first received the baptism of the Holy Ghost. I was filled with the same confidence Philippians 4:13 speaks of: "I can do all things through Christ, which strengthens me."

It's truly amazing when God answers our prayers. After I praised Him fervently, God spoke again very clearly and said, "Now, share this with first ladies from every denomination, nationality, and every corner of the world–to present and future first ladies." He told me to let you know that all God's ministries are important but the position of a first lady is sacred. You are to make being a first lady a priority and put your all into it because all eyes are on you. Most importantly, God's eyes are forever on you. I then asked God how I would convey this message and He said, "Write a book."

When we first began our ministry, my husband was very certain about pastoring. God had spoken to him and said it was time to leave. At the time, however, I couldn't quite understand what was taking place. Don't get me wrong; I always knew we would be Pastor and First Lady; it just wasn't exactly how I envisioned. I didn't expect us to begin the way we did–in our home. Several friends from our former church went on to start their ministries in real buildings. Everyone's assignment is uniquely stamped by Christ so I was in no way comparing our journey to others. But starting church at home seemed so antiquated and I struggled to get past this. I knew God can do anything, but I felt growing a church from home would be difficult. I thought it would have been best if we took some time to look for a church building first.

Sometimes a man of God can outstay his welcome. If you're doing all you can to help build someone else's ministry with your finances, knowledge, presence, prayers, and abilities but nothing you do is right in the leader's eyes, pray about it. Continue to pray until you hear from heaven. If God instructs you to leave, you shouldn't hesitate! Run to the next big assignment God has for you. This is what my husband did.

Oh, You Mean Downstairs...

Every Sunday morning, God would wake him up early. He would wake up my daughters and me and we would get dressed for Sunday service in our family room. I would notice him all dressed up and ask, "Oh, good, have you decided to go visit another church today?"

He would look at me with a puzzled expression and say, "No, we are having our own church service right in our own church."

I would say, "What church? Oh, you mean downstairs in my family room?"

He would respond, “It’s God’s church in our family room, and if you have a problem with this, you can go and talk to God as you leave.”

This conversation played like a broken record every Sunday for several months until God blessed us with a church building. I can truly say that during this period of our ministry, we argued more than we did in all of the nineteen years we had been married. I just couldn’t comprehend why we had to start our ministry this way and why my husband could not understand my feelings. I’m the one who had to listen to our three daughters complain and moan constantly. I am the one who had to share this news with my father when he asked me if we had to travel far from our home to our church. I would then have to repeat myself several times when each family member asked the same thing. I would simply tell them we couldn’t have gotten any closer. At the same time, our phone was ringing off the hook with calls from saints inquiring about our church location. I was too embarrassed to tell them we had no church building; service was being held in our home. When asked how many members we had, I would simply say our congregation was still growing, instead of saying only my family.

My Mother’s Reflection

During this time, I was constantly reminded of my parents. I was living the life of my mother and my daughters were living my childhood. My husband couldn’t see the problem just as my father did not see his. Girls often marry men like their fathers; it’s just something we do. Our husbands may not have all of our fathers’ trademarks but check your husband really good, ladies. I am not saying it is a bad thing because if I could change one thing about marrying my husband, it would be to marry him much sooner than I did. One day, I looked in the mirror and saw my mother's reflection. Reliving her struggles was something I didn't sign up for, but I was in too deep when I came to this realization.

Sometimes as first ladies, we may not quite understand the direction God is taking us through with our husbands. I use the word "through" because when my husband decided to reenlist in the Navy, I had to stop working so I could be there for and with our three daughters. Our girls tried to convince me they would be perfectly fine. We really trust them to do what is right; however, I didn't want to come home from work and see my house transformed into a revolving science lab.

A few months after returning from Afghanistan, God told my husband to start his ministry, which meant one weekend every month, he would not be at church. My thoughts were, "Why not wait to start a church after we have some help?" It just made sense, but for some reason, God wouldn't make my husband grasp this.

First ladies are often placed in challenging situations. The decisions our husbands make–whether personal, business, financial, romantic, or spiritual–all affect us; even if they choose not to mention or inform us of their decisions. When we said our wedding vows to each other before God, we made a decree. When we came together in marital bliss, our souls and spirits became intertwined. Be that as it may, God does not connect our feelings; this is something we as couples have to work hard on together. Occasionally, our husbands may think totally off the charts and wonder why we as wives don't get it. At the same time, we (ladies) can't understand why our husbands don't consider us. This is exactly what was going on between my husband and me. I was already feeling "some type of way" when he told me he was starting our ministry in our home. Plus, he would be missing one Sunday a month. In my eyes, he never counted the cost. He never asked if

I was ready for all of this. Being a pastor's wife was my dream, but timing is everything–emotionally and spiritually.

Put Me Where He Is

He never asked if I was ready for this.

I was not happy with what was happening, so it caused some tension between us. I had to constantly ask God, "Put me where my husband is. Show me how he is thinking, feeling, and seeing." This was necessary because from where I stood, the pieces weren't connecting. As I continued to pray, God revealed that we (first ladies) must be transformed by Him to enter our husbands' worlds. This is why God told me being a first lady is a ministry. Fully embracing this elevates you to a plane where you and your husband can connect on the same level spiritually so God can get the glory.

> Fulfill my joy by being like-minded, having the same love, being of one accord, of one mind. (Philippians 2:2 NKJV)

How many first ladies can relate to what I went through?

At the time, it seemed as if I was the only one compromising. However, through much patience and prayer, I realized each trial was divinely orchestrated to add to my strength and invigorate me to press on.

Has your husband ever asked you this: "If you have so much to complain about why don't you don't just give up being a first lady?" Has he ever asked you what's so hard about dressing up in designer suits, wearing big, expensive hats, luxury shoes with the matching handbags and gloves, and the expensive jewelry he bought you? Has he questioned why are you complaining when you're not doing anything but sitting pretty? Perhaps these statements didn't come from your husbands but rather from some of your lovely church families. Don't be fooled; the ones you don't hear say it are certainly thinking it. If by chance you never experienced this, I can tell you firsthand these types of comments are insensitive and inaccurate. Being a first lady is more than anyone could ever imagine–and then some. The pastors give the sermons but there is so much behind-the-scenes work that often gets placed on the shoulders of first ladies, especially when you have new members. For 10 years, I did everything from leading prayer to being the Sunday school teacher, secretary, hosting shut-ins once a month, head of the women's department, and minister of music.

Just as my mother had to run the church in Berkeley every weekend while my father was running our second church in Bakersfield, I had to run the church while my husband fulfilled his obligations for the naval reserve once a month. I understood how she felt.

Shortly after our church began to grow, one of our choir members would take it upon herself to accept invitations to sing at other churches. Now, following protocol, members are advised to inform their leaders prior to accepting outside engagements. We are not controlling, but as leaders, we are to protect our members. If something goes wrong, members don't hesitate to rush to their leaders for assistance. Then the leaders are the ones who have to step in and help rectify any situation. Like so many others in the church, this young woman did not want to be compliant.

Acknowledge the Molehill

The pastor and I repeatedly reminded her and the entire church about the importance of proper conduct. Nevertheless, our instructions seemed to fall on deaf ears. This young lady insisted on doing what she felt was best and would rather tell church members about her singing engagements than inform the pastor and me. After several months, she finally decided to tell the pastor about her singing engagements but let me show you how the Enemy works. She would come to me only after speaking with the pastor to let me know about her activities, which she had no reason to do. She would say, "I informed the pastor a few weeks ago, so I'm sure he told you about this." I was sure he didn't tell me.

We were trying to teach the church the correct order and all of a sudden, my husband could not remember to keep me updated on what was going on. We had discussed this situation more than I cared to because the young woman was accepting singing engagements so often. Can you see how such a trivial matter can create an issue between you and your husband? I had to finally jam my husband up regarding this little molehill because I could see where the Enemy was trying to take it, but he had to go! My husband was none the wiser or maybe he just didn't want to see it. But I took this small molehill to God before it grew into a mountain.

A trivial matter can create an issue between you.

Now, you may ask why I would bother God with something so insignificant that I should have been able to handle on my own. I have learned that if the source doesn't rectify a conflict after he/she has been made aware, you should go to a higher source. Similarly, if you talk to your spouse about an issue, and he does not correct it, you have a divine order to take it to God and watch Him fix it.

When I discussed this particular situation with my sister and brother over dinner one evening, the first thing my sister said was, "I don't know why you would marry a preacher."

I looked at her and said, "Marrying a man other than a man of God isn't acceptable. I knew I wouldn't be satisfied with one."

She and my brother asked in unison, "What happened to that sister?"

I explained to them God sent her to another church. A couple of years passed, and my husband and I heard her singing at the state convention. If we didn't bother to look at who was behind the mic, we wouldn't have recognized her by the way she sounded. This is where you can use your own imagination. At one point her voice was so distinctive our national bishop recognized her by name for how anointed her performance was.

Chapter 4

WOMAN OF GOD—WHO ARE YOU?

One evening, I was doing something I don't do much of–surfing the internet. As I was scrolling, I came across an article that explained how 76% of first ladies admitted to being depressed. I had to do a double-take and reread the article to make sure I hadn't misread that. When I realized it was a fact, I turned away from the internet again, this time with tears rolling down my face. My husband was sitting at the dinner table eating, and I read the information to him. I said to him, "I don't understand this." I then said to God, "God, I don't understand this. I can't see how 76% of first ladies serving the true and living God can be depressed. Their husbands are holy men of God who inspire their congregations daily to live holy and prosperous lives. They are spending time with these people on a regular basis, hearing their concerns and helping them meet their needs. How could their wives be depressed? These first ladies are precious gemstones. They are priceless rubies and pearls that can't be duplicated."

I say this because each of us has our own special uniqueness that God Himself molded, shaped, and placed within us. I cried to God, "This isn't right, and it certainly isn't Your will. I will not rest until I find a way to help them. Lord, give me a solution that I may share it with the first ladies."

I know what it's like to be surrounded by all of my loved ones and truly know I am loved yet feel lonely. We have all felt lonely at some point in our lives. But depression is a totally different mindset. Such a high prevalence of depression among first ladies is troubling. It means one thing: they are being spiritually attacked by that foul, lowdown, nasty enemy. He happens to have a first name: Leviathan. He comes to bring confusion and twist your words around so by the time they reach their target they cause problems, but I will expose more on him later. Make no mistake. I am very familiar with the following scriptures:

> Forasmuch then as Christ hath offered for us in the flesh, arm yourselves likewise with the same mind: for he that hath suffered in the flesh hath ceased from sin.
> (1 Peter 4:1)

> Thou wilt keep him in perfect peace, whose mind is stayed on thee: because he trusteth in thee. Trust ye in the Lord forever: for in the Lord Jehovah is everlasting strength. (Isaiah 26:3-4)

The first lady's plate is always full, so one may question, "How can I keep my mind stayed on Christ when I have a multitude of other things overwhelming it?" Honey, you can't afford to live this life without keeping your mind stayed on Christ.

I previously mentioned my purpose for writing this book was to encourage all first ladies. We are a part of an elite circle. Let me pause briefly to say, I love each of you dearly. I pray God will grant you everything you ask of Him in this life to make it more beautiful, peaceful, and pleasant because you deserve it. I hope this brings all the current first ladies joy.

Future First Ladies

Now, I want to take a moment to address our future first ladies. Many of you, like me, already know you are destined to be pastors' wives; God has already placed this direction in your spirit. Some of you have accepted the ministry without opposition. Contrarily, the idea of being a first lady may pose a problem for others. Some of you ladies are convinced you really don't have to work in your church. You believe it's enough to show up on Sundays dressed in your new, expensive designer suit with matching hat, designer handbag, stiletto heels, and dripped in jewels. You think as long as your husband preaches the church happy, the members will take care of all the church's needs.

I suggest you begin by searching your heart.

Some first ladies joined under the impression that your titles would somehow grant you love and consideration from everyone you encounter. You feel that all will accept your excuses and love your comments. Perhaps you went in thinking you would be respected by all who knew you. Some of you went in thinking you would be showered with gifts on any given day and chauffeured around town. You thought every church you attend would have a seat reserved with your name on it. Some of you went in thinking that your position as the first lady of your church would make your husband treat you like a first lady–and his *only* lady. If you think so, you will be sorely disappointed–it doesn't quite pan out that way.

Sometimes our husbands will even forget to thank God for us when they speak in church. However, that doesn't change who we are, and we must not let it change our attitudes. We must remember how God made us. God took one rib from Adam to create his one woman. We share bones and flesh together and therefore are one (Genesis 2:22-23).

I was told by a bishop this makes us our husbands' prime ribs. We are top of the line.

Future pastors' wives, know you have a greater advantage over current pastors' wives. Your leverage is that you are now aware of the challenges that come with the ministry. Do not fear. Remember God does not call the qualified; He qualifies those He calls (Romans 8:30). As you embark on this ministry, I suggest you begin by searching your heart and desires. Fast and pray that God will show you what type of woman of God you really are.

Food for Thought

Will you work with your husband 100-plus percent to build a solid foundation for God as He leads your husband?

Are you 100-plus percent willing to share your husband with the congregation if the majority of them are unsaved single women? Are you willing to do so if the majority of men there are homosexuals?

Will you commit to your husband 100-plus percent when the membership is decreasing quicker than it is growing?

Will you use your gifts 100-plus percent to help build the ministry?

Will you continue to be faithful to God 100-plus percent when you are lied on and when people in your inner circle criticize your parenting skills due to the mistakes your children are making?

PART 2

Now That I'm Here

Chapter 5

I DESIRED TO BE A FIRST LADY

In 2008, God blessed me with my childhood dream: to be a pastor's wife. My mother and aunt fostered this dream but unfortunately, neither of them was there to show me the blueprint on how to gracefully step into this position or share with me wisdom on what it means to be a first lady. How do I make this work? How do I help our church grow? These are questions I am sure many first ladies are trying to answer.

The Word of God says to go into the highways and hedges and compel people to come in (Luke 14:23). Commissioned to do this, my husband and I began witnessing and spreading the love of God to the community. We prayed and fasted continually.

When you do this, eventually, a few people may come to fellowship with you. You will be happy and feel inspired because God has heard you and is answering your prayers. Your husband is preaching the Word of God, and you are teaching, singing, and praising the God of our salvation. You are faithful and on time, more often than not.

Unfortunately, it is not all sunshine and roses. Challenges will arise. When the pastor is running late or can't make it to church, you observe how difficult it becomes to get the congregation in one accord.

You notice you can't get the church to pray along with you the same way they do when the pastor is there. They suddenly don't remember the words of the songs you sing, although they are the same songs the pastor sings. Yes, they sing those very same songs exuberantly with him. In fact, they out-sing you with these same songs when the pastor is present.

Honestly, I've never seen so many bad attitudes amongst the saints than when the first lady has to take over in the pastor's absence. When she asks the church to do something, everyone looks at each other as if to say, "Who is she talking to?" or they act as if you said nothing. As a first lady, this will never make you feel good. I don't think anyone would appreciate this type of behavior and frankly, we don't deserve this. So, what do you do?

Accept the Ministry as a Blessing

Once again, you must understand being a first lady is a ministry assigned by God; accept it as a blessing. God has chosen us for this position. Remember those He calls, He qualifies. As first ladies, we must take a moment to reflect on the gifts God has given us. Now, I know all first ladies bear the gift of looking stunning as if we created fashion, but this is not the gift I am speaking about. I'm speaking of the fruitful area in your life, which God has placed inside of you to share with the world.

You may be gifted in singing. It is something you enjoyed and embraced wholeheartedly. Singing is something you looked forward to doing because it allowed you to show up as the best version of yourself. You owned it. It is where God was really using you to get all the glory. You touched lives and were more alive when you sang. You were singing before you met your spouse. In fact, singing was one of the many things your spouse loved about you. Why did you stop after becoming a first lady?

Why did you stop after becoming a first lady?

Maybe you were a teacher. You taught some of the most challenging children and you were awarded for being the best at what you did. Perhaps you were a great musician; you taught more students good music than you can count. Yet, once you became a first lady, your fire dwindled. Did God tell you to stop? If He didn't, find yourself again and get back to using your gifts because nothing anyone else says matters.

Lost Time

Let me share a true story with you. There was a young man who was born and raised in the Church of God in Christ. Let's call him 'Z'. At the age of eleven, he began hanging with the wrong crowd. It was only a matter of time before he started ditching school and smoking. As he grew older, he began selling drugs and would often use them. Eventually, he experimented with stronger narcotics. He and his mother would often admit he spent more time in prison than he did as a free man. He joined a gang and after a period of time, he became one of the gang leaders in prison. By the age of 31, the young man was finally released. He decided it was time to make a change and surrendered his life to God.

After seeing this young man completely alter the trajectory of his life and seriously pursue God, his uncle, who was a pastor, felt he was ready for the next chapter of his life, marriage. His uncle called a family member to see if she knew any young ladies from church who were saved and filled with the Holy Ghost that she could introduce him to. His cousin prayed and asked God to show her who to introduce this young man to. When God answered her prayers, she did not hesitate to introduce them.

They fell in love and in due time, they got married. God blessed both of them with good jobs. Later, God anointed their union, and they became Pastor and First Lady. This came as a complete surprise to both his family and hers. They never doubted God's ability; they were just shocked by His timing and who He chose to use. When you walk according to God's plans, He truly makes up for lost time. It seemed to happen so suddenly. Z surpassed everyone in his family who had been living for the Lord and was waiting to become a pastor.

God's timing is not our timing. I'm reminded of Matthew 20:16, which says, "The last shall be first and the first shall be last. For many are called but few chosen." This young man never thought about being a pastor; his only desire was for God's will to be done in his life. His wife, on the other hand, neither wanted him to be a pastor nor cared to be a pastor's wife. She fought relentlessly even though they were both born in the Church of God in Christ. I made this statement because I personally know several people whose spouses are from different denominations, and their beliefs are like night and day.

Not all Christian women want to be pastors' wives.

Except They Agree

You may feel as long as both of you love God, denominations don't matter. Believe me when I say if your spouse's denomination believes worshiping Mother Mary is the only way you will make it to heaven, while you believe Jesus is the only way, you will undoubtedly have problems. If one denomination says you don't have to attend church to be a Christian, while the other says you must, you will certainly have problems. Furthermore, if one denomination says you must worship God the Father, God the Son, and God the Holy Ghost, while the other says Jesus is only a prophet, this will cause major conflict in your relationship. How can two walk together except they agree? Two people must decide to walk together to have a successful marriage (Amos 3:3).

Admittedly, not all Christian women want to be pastors' wives. They have heard the horror stories and witnessed the disrespect first ladies have to endure. They have seen how the churches stand idly by and let the first lady be hurt and disrespected. Sadly, the truth is some first ladies also wonder why their men, the pastors in charge, are silent when they are being mistreated. As a leader of the church, where are the pastors when this is going on? As the covering for the first lady, why isn't she being protected?

Whatever her reason, Pastor Z's wife in the story did not want that ministry, and she proved it. Her attendance at church was very infrequent. When she did decide to go, she was always very late, refused to take part in the service and would even sit at the very back of the church. On top of that, when service was over, she expected her husband to leave without doing what pastors do: greet the members of the church.

She and her husband were the leaders of a very large congregation that just so happened to be all-white. The only African Americans who attended church were the first family: the pastor, his wife, and their two sons. Could this have been the reason why she didn't want to be a pastor's wife? Maybe being the minority in her own church made her uncomfortable. As Christians, we are all one nation under God and thus, should not see color. We are all serving the same one, true, living God. Love sees no color. When Christ died on the cross, He died for every man, woman, boy, and girl from every nationality, ethnicity, and denomination.

I cannot say definitively what her reason was for not wanting to be a pastor's wife, but she knew. What I know for certain is that being a first lady is not for every woman or the faint of heart. You will not always be happy. Some days it will be hard to wear a smile on your face. You will not always understand what is going on or have all the right answers. You will not always be loved by everyone. You may even find yourself praying, crying out to God, and wondering if He can hear you or if He even remembers you. If you find yourself feeling like this, remember Jesus said He will never leave us or forsake us (Hebrews 13:5).

As Pastor Z continued to preach the gospel and stayed faithful to God, she remained unhappy. This resulted in her distancing herself from their marriage and ministry. Consequently, her attitude hurt her husband and hindered their ministry. God gave them the ministry her husband could really identify with. The majority of the congregation was rehabilitated ex-convicts just as her husband and they really loved him. Maybe if she would have been more receptive to giving and receiving love from the congregation, they would have felt the same toward her. Perhaps the reality of being a leader of a congregation with a criminal past was much more than she had in mind. Was she rejecting God's plan for her life?

She continued to fight with her husband about the ministry and even threatened to leave him. Being the family man that he was, he did not want to lose his family. Not knowing exactly what to do at that point, he just continued praying and fasting. Although his wife saw the hurt in her husband's eyes, it wasn't enough for her. She would not let God fix her heart and solve the problem she had. The Enemy was not going to let this first lady go.

> The thief comes only to steal and kill and destroy; I have come that they may have life, and have it to the full. (John 10:10 NIV)

The Firstborn

Instead of giving her troubles completely over to God, this first lady decided to take matters into her own hands. She was aware her husband had a son from a previous relationship. Pastor Z loved his son more than his own life. His family thought having his son would somehow change him, but it didn't. When his son was born, he was still going in and out of prison.

Years later, when he met his wife, Pastor Z thought it was wonderful; his life was complete. He had a son and now a wife. Unfortunately, his wife didn't care much for the close relationship her husband had with his son. When she got pregnant, and they had their son together, she figured maybe his relationship with his new son would reduce the time he spent with his older son who lived with his biological mother. Now, her husband had two sons he loved equally. Jealousy continued to raise its ugly head as the wife did not want her husband to share his love with his first son the way he did. She decided to take his older son to get a paternity test.

The results came back, and she found out his first son was not his biological child. To make matters worse, she took it upon herself to share that news with her husband. When the entire family became aware, it created chaos. Pastor Z and the entire family were sad and angry, questioning her character as a woman; her actions backfired on her. How could she go behind her husband's back the way she did? To add fuel to the fire, she made sure that both of the sons knew about this. You can imagine what that did to these two children.

In anguish, Pastor Z cried out to God, "What did I do wrong? Why is my life turning out to be such a disappointment? What do I do now?" As time went on, the pastor spent less time with the older son. He began distancing himself more and more until he completely severed ties with his first-born. Having his father exit his life negatively affected the oldest son causing him to venture down the wrong path. The first lady was finally getting what she wanted: her husband and their son alone without his oldest son in the picture.

In the midst of it all, this pastor's wife would not let the news of his oldest son go to rest; she constantly reminded him about it. She knew without a shadow of a doubt her husband would be so disgusted with God that he would resign from being the pastor. Doubt and confusion plagued the pastor's mind. "Where is God while all this is happening? Maybe my wife is right. I should never have become a pastor. I must be doing something wrong." Pastor Z questioned God and the ministry He gave them. The distraught pastor shared his thoughts and feelings with his mentor and former pastor. His mentor faithfully prayed for him and encouraged him to rebuild his relationship with his son.

Chapter 6

YOU CAN'T DO IT ON YOUR OWN

Have you ever felt like giving up? Not on God, but on being a first lady. Imagine meeting your soulmate. You've made plans to get married, start a family, find a good church, and just live out your dreams with the love of your life. Then all of a sudden, God calls you into the ministry. This may not pose a problem for those of us who want to be pastors and first ladies. However, for those who don't, it may be difficult to deal with. Let me make this very clear; you can't do it on your own.

Can you imagine living in this world without living in God's will? Trouble is on every side. Not knowing God as your personal Savior makes life troublesome. You may have people around you but are afraid to share your hurt and pain with them because you don't know if they will judge you. This is how the pastor felt. Can you imagine what it is like not wanting to be a first lady but all of a sudden that position is thrust upon you? You do not want to do it but there's not much you can say to your spouse because God is the one who has called him. Who is he to say no to God? You can say no, but it won't go well.

As first ladies, if we want to avoid messy marriages, we must be open to God's will. We have no excuses (Romans 1:20). Our wills must be God's will. It doesn't matter how we feel or what we think about it. We must always be open to God's will. When we do so, we won't have to worry about getting whipped by Him for disobedience. The Enemy will always come at you with unbelief, envy, strife, and jealousy. None of these things are of God. If you have bitterness, envy, and selfish ambitions in your heart, get rid of it. Don't brag and deny the truth. Such wisdom does not come from above but rather, it is carnal and demonic.

> For where you have envy and selfish ambition, there you find disorder and every evil practice.
> (James 3:16 NIV)

Back to Pastor Z… He continued to pray and fast. God put a deeper desire and a special hunger within him. He took courage in this ministry and grew closer to God. He felt if he stayed connected to God, He would take the hurt away from him. On the other hand, his wife thought after revealing that his oldest son was not his, maybe she would be happy and could focus on their marriage, ministry, and the son they shared. Unfortunately, this didn't happen, and his wife continued to feel left out. She then complained that Pastor Z was putting the church before her and their son.

The arguments continued and she showed up less and less as a first lady. She allowed the Enemy to create strongholds of insecurity, doubt, and unbelief in her life. When these things are in your life, you can be sure sin is on the way. However, when in faith you ask God for help without doubting, He will answer.

> For the one who doubts is like a wave of the sea, that is blown and tossed by the wind. (James 1:6b NIV)

Prayer Warrior

As first ladies, we must be prayerful. As a matter of fact, every first lady must be a prayer warrior. We are blamed for half of the things that go wrong in the church. Therefore, the only way we are going to make it with our husbands, children, and ministries is through prayer (Luke 18:1). The motto at our church is "Much prayer, much power. Some prayer, some power. Little prayer, little power. No prayer, no power." We must realize the Enemy is not playing with us. His whole plot is to graveyard kill us. In any way he can, he will; nothing is off limits.

God calls us to be alert and soberminded watching out for the schemes of the Devil who "prowls around like a roaring lion looking for someone to devour" (1 Peter 5:8). I believe we are living in the last days that the book of Revelation speaks about, and the Enemy knows this. Hence, he influences the churches to war against each other. He causes families to plot against each other and spouses to fight each other.

God's people who are called by His name must humble themselves, pray, seek His face, and turn from their wicked ways. When we do this, He will hear from heaven, forgive our sins, and heal our land (2 Chronicles 7:14). However, if we fail to do as God asks, worse things will happen to us (John 5:14).

God is merciful and great. He means exactly what He says. When God gives instructions to the men and women of God, we must obey. I think as first ladies, we feel the orders God gives to our spouses are solely for them, but that is not true. God's ministry is just as important as our wedding vows. We must be all in it 100%; there is no room for 50/50. When it comes to marriage, God deals with oneness. This is why He said this:

> So they are no longer two, but one flesh. Therefore what God has joined together, let no one separate.
> (Matthew 19:6 NIV)

God feels the same way about the ministries He gives us. We should be working with each other to accomplish His will. But often times the pastor tries to separate his ministry from the first lady. The credential holders in the church want to separate their ministries from the pastor and so forth. This is not the way God designed it to be. He gives the pastor, who is the overseer of the church, the vision for the church. Every ministry within the church is subject to the pastor's vision to build the church. God's orders are not based on feelings or how the situation appears to be. God's orders are to be sought, applied, and executed for His glory and honor (Ephesians 5:25).

Each Member Has a Purpose

The physical body is one but has many members. Each member has a specific purpose for the body to function effectively. This is how it ought to be with the body of Christ. You cannot separate Christ from His church any more than you can separate the head from the body. Jesus is the head of His church (1 Corinthians 12:12).

Regrettably, Pastor Z's wife did not understand her role. As first ladies, we must communicate with our husbands better and come to a mutual understanding. We must stay on our knees in prayer, talking and crying out to God that He may help us accept and want to be a part of His ministry. Be warned that fighting against God's ministry and offending each other will get you in serious trouble with Him. If you go against what God has charged your husband to do or where God has positioned him, you will destroy yourself.

> Do not touch My anointed ones, And do My prophets no harm. (Psalm 105:15 NKJV)

> But whoso shall offend one of these little ones which believe in me, it were better for him that a millstone were hanged about his neck, and that he were drowned in the depth of the sea. (Matthew 18:6)

Pastor Z's wife learned this the hard way. She and her husband continued arguing about the ministry. Her husband spent more time doing the work of God than with her and their son and she continued to feel disconnected from her marriage as their son grew older. This was perfect timing for the Enemy to parade–and he did.

Like all first ladies, this lady was gifted. However, instead of owning her gifts, giving them to God, and allowing Him to show her how to use them for His kingdom, she refused to accept her calling.

Sometime later, they received good news from the doctor that they were having another son. Not only were they happy but also both of their families and the entire church family. They hoped it would fix the couple's marital and ministry problems and point them in the right direction. Was God working with them on their marriage? Perhaps her husband would pay more attention to her, and she could rest better knowing he was catering more to her needs.

They hoped it would fix the couple's marital and ministry problems.

After their son was born, the family began attending church together. Their church family was very happy because now, the first lady was showing up more with their two youngest sons. Finally, they had a pastor and first lady together in ministry as they always wanted. As time passed and their sons grew older, her husband returned to his old ways of spending more and more time with the church ministry. Of course, the first lady began complaining once again. She was agitated about him doing too much outreach for the church and not spending enough time with her and their sons. Her unhappiness showed again, and her mother noticed it.

Dropped a Bomb

One day, the first lady confided in her mother and told her the most shocking news: her youngest son was not her husband's. Instead, he belonged to one of the elders in her former church whom she dated before she married her husband. This man was not only married, but he was also a pastor himself. The Enemy stops at nothing to completely strip us of everything we have. Scripture says be angry and sin not. We must not let the sun go down on our wrath (Ephesians 5:26). Getting angry to the point where you are blinded by sin is designed to trip you up and give you a reason to justify your wrongdoings.

Sometimes we don't set out to sin or stay in it for as long as some of us do. However, before we know it, we have not only overstayed in sin, but we find ourselves stuck in it and can't get out as quickly as we got in. The problem with being angry is that we usually don't know how far to go.

God is merciful, and He allows us to get angry. This is a choice we make. We are humans. We operate in the flesh and will make mistakes. These are just a few excuses we make for justifying why we sin. However, remember what Jesus said:

> Be ye therefore perfect, even as your father which is in heaven is perfect. (Matthew 5:48)

This verse simply instructs us to be complete. You must reach a personal level of maturity. God knows and understands this. He also understands we cannot win the fight against the Enemy without Him. This is why with all of His love, He instructs us to acknowledge Him in all our ways, and He shall direct our paths (Proverbs 3:5-6).

Soul Snatcher

Adultery affects so many people. This is a fact. Someone always gets hurt, and it is often the innocent spouse. The Enemy will never show you the results of sin. He only shows you its fleeting pleasures. It is not in his nature to ever display what will happen after sin has finished its dirt. He doesn't care.

You must reach a personal level of maturity.

Sin comes for one purpose, but before it concludes this one purpose, it will steal everything you have worked hard for. It will take away your fasting, praying, studying God's Word, and church attendance, but that is not all. Inevitably, you will lose your peace, love for God and others, spirit of happiness, and desire for more of God. Satan snatches your soul! Then, there's nothing left but death. This is how the Enemy operates. His ultimate goal is always death.

I can't begin to understand how the first lady must have felt keeping such a painful secret to herself all those years. She must have pondered many times about the right time to open up. Of course, there is nothing good about sin but to expose it. Can you imagine how her mind was in turmoil racing back and forth? This situation would affect her family, her husband's family, her older son, the pastor she shared her son with, his wife, his family, his in-laws, both congregations, and others.

Her mother was close friends with her mother-in-law. They had known each other for years before they became in-laws. Her mother was shocked and hurt. She knew it was only a matter of time before the news would spread to her son-in-law's family. She continued to pray that her daughter's actions wouldn't cause irreparable damage to their family. How do you deal with a situation like this? Where do you even begin?

If ever the first lady needed God, it was now. Her life was about to change forever. Sure enough, people began to talk. The pastor and father of her love child reached out to the husband's family. It turned out he knew some of them very well. He scheduled a meet-up and told the truth that he was actually the father of the couple's third son.

You Don't Want To Meet the Man I Was

He spoke so boldly about the situation, almost bragging. You would think his title as a husband and pastor would cause him to feel at least an ounce of remorse for the infidelity that led to him having child with another man's wife, but there was none.

As the family member listened to his story, she was disgusted. She had to remind him that the innocent spouse was not only a pastor, but also an ex-convict and ex-gang member. Now, despite how holy each of us is, everyone has a past. Anyone can revert to their old ways as sin is merely lying dormant within us. That's why we must die to our flesh daily.

How do you deal with a situation like this?

No one wanted to see the other side of him before he became a pastor. The family member informed the boasting pastor that his actions and cocky attitude would not produce anything good. The gravity of the situation finally hit him. His demeanor changed instantly, and he immediately began to ask God for direction on how to handle the situation. He knew that all of their lives were about to change.

Against her better judgment, the first lady's mother decided not to say anything. Can you imagine all of the heaviness her mother was carrying trying to help her daughter keep this deep, dark secret from her husband? This brewing disaster was slowly coming to a boil. Once her secret was exposed, many people would be hurt and ashamed. Imagine how their congregation would respond to the news.

Honesty Is the Best Policy

Honesty is always the best policy; it is the only way we will see God. Often times telling the truth is easier said than done. When faced with turbulent times like these, you must activate your inner Bible scholar. Search your heart and remember God will never leave you or forsake you, even when it seems there is no hope. Look to the hills from whence your help comes. Know that it comes from the Lord. Unfortunately, the first lady's mother could not bring herself to tell her friend, the husband's mother the truth.

> Be not deceived; God is not mocked: for whatsoever a man soweth, that shall he also reap. (Galatians 6:7)

Eventually, her friend heard the truth from a family member. The pastor's mother was very worried about how her son and grandsons would take the news. Her son had overcome so much. As mentioned earlier, before he became a pastor, Z was in and out of the prison and using drugs for the majority of his life. His mother, along with the rest of her family had been praying and fasting for him to give his life to the Lord. He finally surrendered to the Lord in his late thirties.

He fell in love with a Christian woman–the only Christian woman he had ever dated. God had blessed him with three sons. God anointed him to become a pastor over a church he did not have to start. His church was full of people who loved him, his wife, and children. He didn't lack anything. His transformation was remarkable.

Nobody expected him to ever give his life to the Lord or get married. But God looks beyond our faults and sees all of our needs (Romans 5:8). We serve a God who takes our filthy lives and cleans them up. He will anoint us and put us in places our minds cannot begin to imagine.

His mother knew the truth could potentially set her son back so she couldn't bring herself to deliver the blow to him. Instead, she asked her niece if she would tell him the sad news that his youngest son was not his biological son. Initially, her niece was hesitant not wanting to be involved, but after fasting and praying, she agreed.

Finally, she told him and as expected, Pastor Z was distraught, broken, and angry. Nevertheless, in spite of opposition, he did not let his feelings deter him from God's promises. He continued to live his life as normal. For several years, he tried hard not to let this change his feelings for his wife and son. He remained a pastor and stayed with his wife. Their families kept praying they could move past this. They were really trying to turn the next page, but the Enemy didn't appreciate it at all.

Completely Overwhelmed

One day, the first lady received a phone call from the hospital that her husband was involved in an accident at work that had almost severed his arm. By the time his wife arrived at the hospital, the nurses had already sedated him with narcotics. She wasn't able to warn the doctor about his history. The doctors had dropped the ball, not seeing the cautionary notes of his history on file. Upon discharge, one of the doctor's orders was he wasn't allowed to operate heavy machinery. This meant he could no longer work or drive himself around.

The news did not stop him from pastoring, he just had to rely on his wife to drive them to church. You can imagine this didn't go over well; her attendance record at church was practically nonexistent at this point. She also wanted to control her husband's attendance. She felt he should not attend church as much as he wanted to. Their marriage took a blow again, and they returned to their old ways of arguing. Despite his history with substance abuse, he followed the doctor's orders and took his prescription for pain. Eventually, he became completely overwhelmed by all the turmoil.

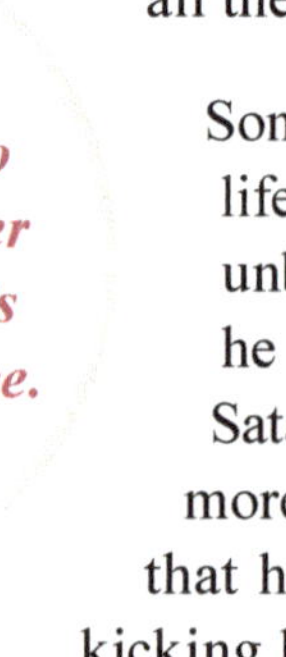

She wanted to control her husband's attendance.

Sometimes, the circumstances of life can weigh you down and seem unbearable. Just when he thought he had reached his lowest point, Satan began tormenting him even more. The very details of his life that he tried to rise above started kicking him. Every day, it seemed as if he had to relive the fact that his wife did not want to be a first lady and that two of his sons weren't his biologically.

Everywhere he turned, he was reminded of how his wife had cheated on him and had a baby by another pastor. The news had spread like wildfire. How could he face his congregation?

Living in shame, he decided to resign as the pastor and returned to his position as elder at his former church with his uncle. His wife was a happy woman again because he was no longer a pastor. Now, she was not obligated to go to church or serve there; however, that was not the end of the misery. His wife soon got uncomfortable when he started working hard in the church and became just as faithful as he was before. She fought with him about his diligent work in the church and this reignited the problem in their marriage.

Repeating history, his wife stopped going to church as often as she would. The Enemy seized the prime opportunity to destroy her husband with shame and embarrassment. This caused him to relapse, and he ended up getting addicted to the prescribed medication. As his addiction grew, his presence in church lessened. It ultimately drove a wedge between him and his wife and they separated.

Triumph and Tragedy

This split allowed him to rebuild his relationship with his three sons. The four of them had an amazing relationship and began to attend church together. The three sons bonded as brothers, and he taught them that regardless of what anyone said about them, they were his sons. He and his three sons continued attending church until he passed away at the age of sixty-three. His passing was very tragic. The first lady had lost her husband. Her sons had no father. The church where he pastored and led so many to Christ was left without their beloved leader.

This brings me back to the question: "How did I get here?" When God gives you the ministry of being a first lady and you refuse this position, you should 1. ask Him to forgive you for not seeing it as a blessing. Ask God to create a clean heart in you and renew a right spirit within you (Psalm 51:10). Or 2. have enough respect for God and leave the ministry.

> So, because you are lukewarm—neither hot nor cold—I am about to spit you out of my mouth.
> (Revelations 3:16 NIV)

One of my uncles shared with his wife that God had called him to be a pastor. His wife did not want anything to do with being a pastor's wife. She decided to leave my uncle in order to not be a hinderance to him and the ministry. It is better to do this than to ruin a good ministry, your family, and the church family. Remember, God will never force himself on anyone.

Pastor Z's wife should have just accepted the ministry God gave her. She should have asked God for help to forget all of the negative things she heard and thought about being a first lady. Remember what I said about our unique gifts? Perhaps, she could have owned her gift and used it to contribute to the ministry. If she had trusted in the Lord with all her heart, refused to lean on her own understanding, and acknowledged God in all her ways, He would have directed her path (Proverbs 3:5-6). The Enemy would not have had a crack to squeeze through.

I don't want you to think I am blaming the first lady for what happened to their marriage and ministry because God certainly didn't recruit me to be a judge. One thing I know for certain is it may only take one person to destroy a marriage, but it takes two to make a marriage right; it takes two to make it out of sight.

I've noticed that pastors can become so immersed in their ministries they simply don't remember to keep their wives connected with what is going on. There has to be a balance between the marriage and the ministry to avoid disconnection between the couple, which makes the wife feel uneasy and unappreciated. When this happens, it is open season and all fair game. If you listen to the Enemy, he will welcome you with open arms.

Chapter 7

HELP ME TO KNOW MY FRIENDS

My mother would always remind me, "Don't be so heavenly-minded that you are no earthly good." First ladies must stay connected to their husbands. Our marriages depend on it. Our families count on it. The ministries God put us in charge of rely on it. For this reason, we must go back to God and repent for not working diligently in our ministries as first ladies.

It took me nine years to understand my ministry as a first lady. I would constantly complain to God because I didn't understand why with such a small congregation, the members of the church would let the Enemy use them to cause me trouble. Some of them would ignore me, fail to acknowledge my presence, and not say anything to me. Yet, they would talk for hours with the pastor.

I remember an elder's wife openly starting an argument with me in front of the other church members, visiting pastors, and first ladies. She allowed the Enemy to cause her to be rude and disrespectful. As she was doing this, I was praying inside my spirit asking God to show me how He wanted me to deal with her and what to say to her. If I hadn't taken full control of the situation as God led me to, it would have gotten really bad very quickly. However, I allowed the Holy Spirit to show me how to deal with the Enemy and just what to say to that spirit in the right tone. That Enemy shut up and went away from me. Our guests sat down quietly for the rest of the night, and it turned out to be a wonderful service.

> He shall call upon Me, and I will answer him; I will be with him in trouble; I will deliver him and honor him. (Psalm 91:15 NKJV)

A week later, she, her husband, their two children, and her mother left our church by way of a text message. God answered my prayer. By no means did I pray them away; I just prayed that God's will be done. I prefer to be a leader over a few faithful members than many disruptive members. We don't always enjoy the outcome of God's answers, but we know He answers. When He speaks to us, we must respond, "Your will be done."

First ladies must not let the Enemy come in and take over their ministries. Now that I understand this ministry, I do not give the Enemy any space! Let me say it again: do not give the Enemy any space! I know he will try to make a no-nonsense, tiny nothing into a huge something. But don't give him any opportunities to work (Ephesians 4:27).

I do not give the Enemy any space!

Discover your gift and use it for the glory of God. It does not matter if an auxiliary in your church is up and running well. If the auxiliary is doing what you are gifted in, it needs you, and you need the auxiliary. You can always go outside of your church and start something new or enhance what is already there with your husband. Or you can get involved with something that has already started.

Stay Connected

Never sit in your own church and not be a great part of it. Never let anyone stop you from participating in anything you want to be a part of. Remember who you are and who God has made you to be. You are the first lady; own it! Only one first lady is in your church and that is you. If there are two first ladies in the church, something is wrong and out of order. That's not God's church. If God wanted the church to have two first ladies, He would not have told the men of God to have one wife (1 Timothy 3:2).

As a first lady, you represent:

- The Most High King of kings and Lord of lords
- Your pastor (husband)
- Your family
- Your church
- Future first ladies

Remember, people are like their priests. As first ladies, we must have positive attitudes and be energetic and full of love toward every soul, regardless of what some think of us or how they treat us. We are all adamant about being like Christ until our walk is tested (Matthew 5:39). Trust me; I know it is not easy.

I want to share with you what God revealed to me. God told me He judges me as a first lady, not by what others say to me or what they do to me. He judges me by the way I respond to the treatment of others–good or bad. This keeps me in check.

One of the members of our ministry was an evangelist missionary whom my husband and I met when we first moved to Colorado. At the time I wrote this book, we had known her for 24 years. She and I received our evangelist missionary license together, and she was one of our daughters' godmothers.

The Proper Address

Fourteen years later, she and her husband joined the church that my husband and I pastored. By this time, I was also a district missionary. Oddly, for the entire 10 months she was with our ministry, she had a problem calling me first lady or district missionary; she called me by my first name instead. This caused a ripple effect of confusion among the newer saints, and they too began to address me by my first name. Right about now, some of you first ladies may assume that I am caught up in the titles. To that, I say God chose me for this title, so I am going to represent Him with it. I do the work that comes with the title, so I won't apologize for being called first lady. You can feel the same or not.

It's interesting how we call our doctors by their titles. We respect our judges enough to call them by their titles. Why is it that we have problems calling the men and women of God who keep us up in prayer by their titles?

When my husband could not be at church due to his military service, the evangelist missionary would not accept that he left me in charge of the church. Maybe since we received our missionary licenses at the same time, she felt she could continue to address me the way she did before my title changed.

They have difficulty respecting us in our positions.

However, when you grow in God and He elevates you, there is a different calling on your life. Along with that comes a greater expectation. Please don't misunderstand me. We should not think we are better than anyone else, and we certainly should not expect to be treated better than anyone else. Nonetheless, we should be respected as leaders. Just as we are expected to respect everyone we come into contact with, we shouldn't accept anything less.

For whatever reason, people who are familiar with us before God elevates us often have a problem once we step into position as first ladies. They have difficulty respecting us in our positions. Interestingly enough, these same sisters have no problem respecting our husbands in their positions as pastors. This is the type of behavior first ladies must be aware of, but we will never get used to it. Of course, my husband had to constantly remind the evangelist that my positions as the first lady and district missionary were set in stone. As a result of this and other unacceptable tactics, she eventually decided to part from our ministry without notice.

> Let all things be done decently and in order.
> (1 Corinthians 14:40)

I thank God my husband did not allow the Enemy to abuse and disrespect me and the house of God.

Those Who Belong

I have known pastors who let this Jezebel spirit remain in their churches. They let it linger because they are afraid of losing members. They even attempt to justify this by using the scripture that says let the wheat and tares grow together (Matthew 13:24-30). However, the Jezebel spirit is not in the church for the purpose of growing with others. That spirit is there for one thing only: to take over the entire church. If the pastor doesn't remove the Jezebel spirit from the church through deliverance, when that spirit finally leaves, it will take followers along with it.

Sometimes we will not be accepted by those we once called our friends. As long as you are stagnant and not growing like them, they regard you as their dear friend. Once you begin reaching your highest potential in God and your ministry begins to excel, everything changes.

These people really did not belong to our fellowship and that is why they left us. If they did belong, they would have stayed with us. They left so that it might be clear none of them really belonged to us. Those who end their friendship with you as you rise were never your friends. Be of good cheer, first ladies. Only those ordained by God should remain in your life (1 John 2:19).

PART 3

Stay Focused

Chapter 8

HOW TO IDENTIFY AND CONQUER LEVIATHAN

Why in the world would I still want to be a first lady? My mother who was a first lady for all of my younger life went to be with the Lord separated from the love of her life. Yet, she went to glory doing what she loved most: utilizing and sharing all of her God-given gifts in the ministry of God. She was so focused and dedicated to the love of God that nothing and no one could stand in her way. I realize I must be three times as focused and dedicated as she was.

I mentioned to you earlier about a lowdown, nasty, foul spirit named Leviathan. I'm going to introduce you to him. He is someone you must remember for the rest of your life. Have you ever found yourself working on a project you know was assigned by God? You were so excited about it you couldn't help but share your delight with your husband and church family. Everything was working according to God's plan, then suddenly, the bottom fell out from under it. All those who said they were on board seemingly jumped ship and with no reasonable explanation. This is Leviathan.

Have you ever made a specific point in a conversation and the person you were talking with agreed and then out of the blue the conversation went left? You and the person no longer agreed on anything you were initially talking about. This is Leviathan.

Have you ever been focusing on something and as soon as you were ready to put it into perspective you forgot the point or got confused? This is Leviathan. He is a foul spirit that comes to destroy everything God has stamped His approval on. His purpose is to confuse you and steal your peace. Everything wrong he tries to make seem right. He calls good evil and evil good.

The Key to Overcoming

I have found the key to overcoming Leviathan is knowing who I am in Christ and who Christ is in me. All signs point to the Lord being my solid rock, fortress, rescuer, and protector. I take refuge in Him. He is my shield, salvation, strength, and place of safety (Psalm 18:2). God has placed an abundance of anointed gifts within first ladies that we cannot begin to fathom. However, we must remember who we serve, who we are, and what we have. Leviathan should be afraid to cross our paths.

We are very aware of the fact that some first ladies can preach better than their husbands. That is a gift God has placed within you to help build the ministry He has given to you and your husband. It's not there for you to boast about or belittle your husband with. Do not compete against your husband. Love, encourage, and assure him of your love and admiration for what he does and who he is.

Do not be tricked by Leviathan. Always be vigilant because he brings filthy, lowdown jealousy with him. He will make you feel as if you do not have anything good to bring to the table. Perhaps you have gotten older, a few sizes bigger, or down to the size where your husband has nothing to hold onto. Now when your husband talks to you, it seems as if he won't even look at you.

I want to assure you the problem is not you. The problem is not your husband. The problem is Leviathan. You can take him down by staying on your knees before God and consecrating yourself to fasting. Always use Scriptures to defeat him. These are our greatest weapons to fight and beat him with.

> For the weapons of our warfare are not carnal but mighty in God for the pulling down strongholds, casting down arguments and every high thing that exalts itself against the knowledge of God, bringing every thought into captivity to the obedience of Christ, and being ready to punish all disobedience when your obedience is fulfilled. (2 Corinthians 10:4-6 NKJV)

Imagine your district superintendent presents you with the offer of being a district missionary. What an honor this is. After you and your husband pray about it, you get God's blessing about the position. You and your husband are in agreement about the position and share the news with the district superintendent. Following protocol, the superintendent makes the state supervisor of the women's department aware of his decision to select you.

Blockers

Surprisingly, she tells the superintendent that as long as she is the supervisor of the women's department of that state, you will never be a district missionary. When the superintendent questions her remark, she never gives a legitimate reason. As a matter of fact, she makes it a point to openly let the mothers from your former church of 18 years know that she disapproves of you. She also knows without a shadow of a doubt that this message will be passed on to you firsthand.

How would you feel? Wouldn't you be hurt and distraught? Of course! Perhaps you would never accept another invitation to be a district missionary. You are left with no idea as to why this supervisor felt the need to block you from this position. As far as you are concerned, everything was good between you two. Whenever you saw her, you would extend greetings with hugs and smiles and engage in friendly conversation. You always complimented her, and she would reciprocate. Imagine all this time I looked at her as a mother in Christ and I thought she looked at me as a daughter in Christ. How wrong I was to think she thought of me the same way.

Hurt and disillusioned, you go down on your knees and pray constantly about this issue. You are reminded of Matthew 18:15-17, which says if your brother or sister sins against you, go and point out his or her fault just between the two of you. You ask your Father for advice on how to handle this situation. He advises you not to fight but to leave it alone and let God take care of it. However, you feel the need to know why she acted that way. On three separate occasions, you go to Him again, hoping He would change His mind and give you permission. Each time, He declines. He says if she had a reason, she would have shared it with everyone. Plus, you should never chase down confusion or a lie.

God Justifies

One year later, you are again offered the position of a district missionary by another district superintendent. Once again, you pray about it before accepting the position. You did not know it at the time, but your former bishop and wife had agreed with the superintendent's request for you to be his district missionary. Despite the obstacles, you eventually become a district missionary. You don't have to question others' decisions; your gifts will make room for you (Proverbs 18:16).

The preceding scenario tells my story. I have been the district missionary since 2013. My husband is now a district superintendent. My former bishop and pastor would always say to us: "Ain't nobody God but God."

> What shall we then say to these things? If God be for us, who can be against us? He that spared not his own son, but delivered him up for us all, how shall he not with him also freely give us all things? Who shall lay anything to gods elect? It is God that justifieth.
> (Romans 8:31-33)

The sooner the body of Christ understands and accepts what is written in the above verse, the sooner the love and respect for all first ladies will return. I truly believe when we exercise our gifts to the fullest as God has given us, and we learn to perfect them, there will be no room to harm or offend one another. We must embrace and encourage each other's gifts.

As first ladies, we have several things in common. One of them is being pastors' wives. Moreover, we are the first ladies of the churches God has appointed our husbands to lead. Everyone else comes second.

Ride or Die

We should be our husbands' loudest cheerleaders and most discreet critics. We must keep it real with love and in love–no hidden agendas. We should be our husbands' ride or die and never have to lie.

Sometimes, we find ourselves compromising when it comes to our husbands, children, family members, and close church family. They think when excuses are necessary, they can ask their first ladies to help them out. Thus, we find ourselves making small, no harm excuses. Romans 1:19-23 talks about excuses. They are dressed-up lies we should not engage in.

We are living in a time when first ladies are tapping into their God-given gifts to use for the body of Christ. First ladies are now beginning to feel comfortable prophesying to the church, laying hands on the sick, and preaching in the pulpit. They are comfortable managing the administrative arm of the church and being in charge when the pastor is away. They are getting confident enough to be authors and producers. We are finally where God has been waiting for us to be. We are now in a place to better help the ministry. Keep in mind; it doesn't mean we will be welcomed by all with open arms.

Some of your husbands will be jealous of the anointing that flows in your life. Some of your husbands will be angry because your offering is much more than theirs or that you can get a louder "Amen" from the congregation compared to him. You must remain prayerful and humble and maintain a spirit of submission (Ephesians 5:22). Being submissive does not mean you are to be abused physically, emotionally, verbally, sexually, financially, or otherwise. It does not mean you are his modern-day slave.

Being submissive does not mean you are to be abused.

When you are speaking at church, invite your husband to join you in praying for the saints during the altar call. When it's time to receive your offering, simply request that it is given to your husband, and he will give it to you. Be sure to buy him a nice suit, a pair of alligator shoes, or his favorite ice cream. Get your husband's input when the congregation wants your advice. Do what is necessary to live in peace with your husband (Romans 14:19).

Havoc Wreaker

There is another spirit first ladies should be aware of; his name is Belial. When Belial comes to visit, he will try to wreak havoc in our lives, but we can send him back to the pits of hell where he belongs. First, you must attack him with God's Word. Say, "No weapon formed against me shall prosper" (Isaiah 54:17). Tell him greater is God in you than the tiny Enemy in the world (1 John 4:4). Then you serve the Devil notice by standing in agreement with your husband.

A pastor and wife ended their Sunday service, went home to have a quick dinner with their children and then left home to attend another church service. On their way home from the second service, they began to argue and did so until they were about three blocks away from home. The pastor, who was driving, stopped the car, got out, and made his wife get out of the car as well. Then he got back into the car and drove off. His wife had to walk home all dressed up with her hat on and stiletto heels. She was shocked, angry, and humiliated.

She contemplated what she would do to take revenge. She thought about packing up, taking her kids, and leaving him. It even crossed her mind she should call her family, his family, the bishop, and church family to let them know how cruel he was. Or she should call 911 and have him arrested for making her get out of their car and walk home in her stilettos. She also thought about having their cars towed. But as she was walking planning her revenge, God said not to do anything; He will take care of him. She was so furious she told the Lord she wanted to take care of him herself.

When she arrived home, she received a message on her phone asking her if she could begin orientation that same week for the job she had been waiting for. All of her plans to punish her husband had to be put on the back burner.

The following Sunday, five members of their church quit. The pastor was devastated. Make no mistake; the first lady was hurt when the wife of the family of four told her it was the last Sunday, she, her husband, and their two children would be attending church. The first lady felt the reason this member gave her for leaving was minor and simple to fix, but there was no way they could talk them into staying. At least, this family told them they were leaving. The fifth member, who was one of the first members to join the church left the same Sunday the pastor put the first lady out of their car to walk home. She never said anything to them. It was nine years before they ever heard from this member again.

The first lady felt the pastor brought it on himself. At that point, she could not care less. If he had not put her out of the car, this wouldn't have happened. Of course, she played her part. The pastor wasn't arguing alone. The first lady was exchanging more than a few words with her husband. There were plenty of times when she could have driven away and left him walking. But she never did.

Keeping It 100

Let's keep it real. Our conversations with our husbands are not always hallelujah and bless His holy name. It is not a sin as a first lady to have heated arguments with your husband as long as you don't harm each other. Ephesians 4:26 says to be angry and sin not; let not the sun go down upon your wrath. There is a way to handle conflict. You both talk about it. You both come to an agreement. You both forgive each other.

You both make all the way up, which should be a beautiful make up.

My mother shared with me about a time when she and my father had argued after they came home from church one night. My father went to bed. Later on, after she had put my sisters and brothers to bed, she went to bed and tried to sleep, but she couldn't. She tossed and turned as my father lay sound asleep. She said a few hours had passed, but she still could not fall asleep.

Finally, she asked God why she could not rest like my father. God spoke very clearly and said He was giving her a chance to ask my father to forgive her for arguing with him. She could not understand why she needed to ask my father for forgiveness when he went to sleep without asking her for forgiveness. God said to her that if she did not ask him for forgiveness, she would die. She had no idea if God was speaking about dying naturally or spiritually, but either way, she didn't want to die. So she woke my father up immediately and asked him to forgive her. My father told her he did not think about it anymore after they had finished arguing. He told her that everything was alright. Then he went back to sleep, and she also fell asleep. She said that was the best sleep she could remember ever having.

Open Affection

As we stay focused, we must keep our husbands in plain view. This means we must have balance. Our time with our husbands is very important. Both parties require undivided attention. Don't check your email and text when you are spending time together. Being at church with your husband is not personal time; it's shared time. We need one-on-one quiet, blow in each other's ears, warm, hugging, kissing time. We need one-on-one look into each other's eyes communication time.

All cellphones must be turned off. Texting is off-limits. We need dating time together alone. Our children should see us laughing together and touching each other.

I have only seen my parents touch each other once. That was when my mother tried tickling my father on his side. My father moved her hands away and said to her, "G'on woman and stop." Some of my siblings and I were watching at the time. We were not sure if he was serious or if he was just shy and did not want us to see his playful side. My father was very strict. My mother would often tell him he was so strict God would not live by his rules.

According to *The Five Love Languages* by Gary Chapman, touching is one of the five love languages for husbands and wives. It is a way of communicating emotional love. My second daughter was born prematurely weighing only three pounds. As a result, she had to stay in the hospital for 21 days. My two-year-old daughter and I stayed at the hospital five days a week for about 10 to 12 hours a day. On weekends, my husband would stay for a few hours on Saturdays and a couple of hours after church on Sundays. I would go back to the hospital and stay until he returned from church on Sunday nights.

Our daughter's doctor told me she was releasing our baby from the hospital after 21 days because I was always at the hospital with her and the entire time I was there, I was holding her. I would talk and sing to her. She said there were babies in the nursery who had been there months before our daughter arrived and would still be there when she left because they were not being held and touched. Our daughter was doing better because of the love and affection she received. Can you imagine what would happen if pastors and first ladies touched each other more? Do you know it would positively impact our children and others when they see us

Touching is a way of communicating emotional love.

showing sincere affection to each other? The Enemy would not have a chance on the earth to touch our marriages.

Take Family Vacations

That brings me to my next point. Pastors, wives, and children should take vacations together. Please don't get it twisted. Attending a church convention is not a vacation. Going to a business meeting is not a vacation. It is not fair for pastors, wives, and their children to spend three to four days in church and the rest of their time counseling others or tending to other church business. If you only see and talk to your family when you are in church or on your way to or from church, you have a problem.

Sit down with your children and plan a vacation. Most pastors will go along with whatever you choose because they usually don't want to have anything to do with the planning. Check your husband's schedule and work around his time when planning. Let him know it is family time.

If he is not interested, go on vacation without him. That will not look good for him and the church. Church families love to see pastors, first ladies and their children spending quality family time together. Church families want to know that their leaders are together and happy as one big family. This gives them hope and a wonderful life to look forward to. They know that just as God blessed their leaders, He will also bless them. They will look forward to a wonderful life, which in faith will soon come.

Take Time Alone Together

As much as you love your children, you need to get away from them at some point to be alone with your spouse. In fact, you need one-on-one time with your husband away from everyone and everything. Go to a place where no one knows you, and you don't know anyone. If you decide to sleep in all day and have room service, do so. If you decide to take a bubble bath all day and a warm flowing shower all night with no interruptions, you can.

Husbands and wives really need to reconnect; let us commit to being better communicators. Make sure the dreams you shared together are still the ones you are working toward. Sometimes we can be so consumed with church obligations we forget we are soulmates. We are still "Bone of my bones and flesh of my flesh; she shall be called woman, because she was taken out of man" (Genesis 2:23).

This is not a way to get our husbands to neglect their obligations to the church. That's not the goal. Pastors must fulfill their duties to the church, and we should support them. However, they also have a duty to us, their wives. They are to love us as Christ loved the church. What an amazing comparison. Christ loves the church unconditionally and completely. He gave His life for the church (Ephesians 5:25).

Do not let your husbands convince you that attending a church convention together is your vacation. Don't you dare accept this. You deserve much better. When you return from your vacation, both of you will be rested, rejuvenated, and inspired to press on with the plans God has given to you for the church. First ladies, be careful not to let your husbands go back to being so busy you feel like roommates with children, not husbands and wives.

If you must schedule date night on the calendar, do it. You need it; you deserve it, and God is pleased with it. Show love and be happy! As you enjoy yourselves remember you know who you see, but you don't know who sees you. Keep it classy and be Kingdom-minded.

Take Time for Yourself

Now that we have discussed family vacations, let's talk about you. You deserve a vacation of your own. If you can't get away for an entire week, go somewhere for the weekend. Take a spa day and stay at a nice hotel with room service. If you do not want to do anything but stay in your room and lay in bed all day, that's fine. It is your vacation. Everything should be done on your terms. Give your family restrictions. Do not let them call you nonstop; you call them. Learn how to enjoy you.

Chapter 9

SILENT STRUGGLES

When you make up your mind to stay focused, every enemy will come at your family. Let's keep it real. You know as well as I do that first ladies are blamed for everyone who leaves the church. We are blamed if our husbands are late for church or if they could not quite get their message to the standard it should be. We are blamed for our children if they stray from the will of God.

My older sisters and brothers shared stories with me about some of the unfortunate circumstances they had to encounter. The church blamed my mother for everything. My second oldest brother was born with polio. All my mother and father could do was consistently pray for him. My mother would try to keep him still because he wanted to do what he saw his other brothers and sisters doing. All eyes were on my mother as if his condition was somehow her fault. But she fasted and prayed and prayed and fasted until one day, God completely healed him.

When my oldest brother was three years old our family dog had to pull him out of the pond in my grandmothers back-yard. My mom was devastated when she heard about this. God being as merciful as He is, allowed no harm upon my brother.

My oldest sister swallowed a piece of glass when she was three years old. At this time, my parents were living in Bakersfield, California.

No doctors there could help, so they had to drive to Los Angeles. In 1943, they had to travel down a one-way lane. The doctors were able to remove the glass from her throat and God healed her. The church also blamed my mother for this incident.

A few years later, my second oldest sister who was five years old at the time was cleaning the kitchen stove and it caught on fire. As a result, she suffered from third-degree burns. God totally blessed her because you would never know it if you look at her. Again, the entire church blamed my mother. My mother constantly heard the whispers from the saints questioning her parenting skills.

A year later, my brother who was healed from polio sustained severe bites to his head by the neighbor's pit bull. Who did the church blame? My mother, of course. The church certainly didn't think she was a good mother. They even questioned why my father made her their first lady. My mother had to listen to all of the bad talk about her and her children. However, the church never had anything bad to say about my father.

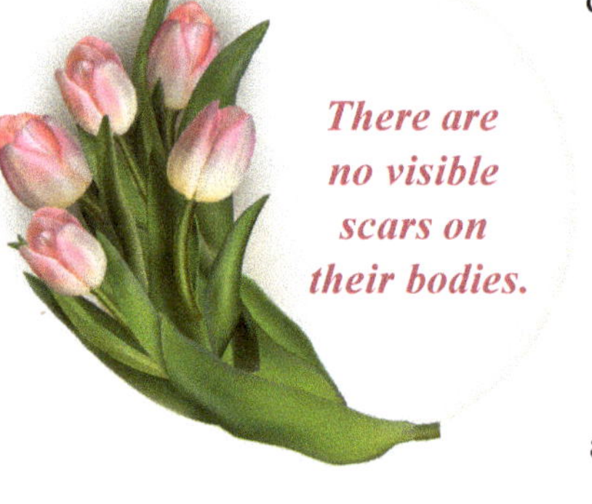

God healed all of my siblings who were injured. There are no visible scars on any of their bodies. All the church believed was that my mother let these accidents happen to her children. What they never knew was that my mother had to get a job because my father would spend his money on the church leader. Instead of taking his hard-earned money to buy groceries and clothing for my mother and their children, he would buy groceries and clothes for other families. All the other members of the church were contributing to the leader as well.

When all of the accidents happened with my older sisters and brothers, my father was no longer an assistant pastor. He had begun pastoring his own church. My mother was truly a God-fearing woman. People would see her holiness as a sign to take advantage of her, including my father.

My father and uncle were both pastors and business partners. When payday came, my uncle would pay all the other workers and tell my father he didn't have enough money to pay him. He would tell my father if my mom ran out of food let her go next door and get some from his wife. His reasoning was that my parents were pastor and pastor's wife, so they shouldn't mind the other workers being taken care of first even if that meant we had to borrow food. That was my mom's own brother; can you imagine that?

The Unwritten Rule

My sister shared with me one of the silent struggles my mother endured. My sister was always a curious kid and when she would hear my mother crying, she would peek inside the room, and see my mother throwing the notes away. My mother would prepare my father's church suits, and in his pockets, she would regularly find notes with names, phone numbers, and addresses from different women in the church. Unlike most women, my mother never approached or mentioned this to anyone. Had my sister not been snooping in her trash, she would have never known. Instead, my mother remained prayerful and continued to be the wife she vowed to be.

Most people, from the world to within the church walls have no idea what we go through as first ladies. Truth is we don't really know each other's silent struggles. One thing we know for certain is all of us go through. Unfortunately, we live by this unwritten rule that it is better to cry about it than to talk about it. I pray you find someone to share

your feelings with, someone to open up to about your hurts, concerns, and problems, someone you can trust.

Hold Your Peace

There was a time when there was discord between my state supervisor and me. Usually, she would freely call me when it came to discussing money. In this particular instance, however, she did not extend me the same courtesy but went directly to the district superintendent and complained to him. I guess she thought going over my head would get her some "results." However, my superintendent told her to discuss her concerns with me directly.

By the time she got around to talking to me, my husband had become my superintendent and suddenly, whatever was so bothersome to her became insignificant. Being disrespected by your leaders is never a good feeling. But Exodus 14:14 says the Lord Himself will fight for you, so just stay calm and hold your peace.

Unfortunately, people would rather seek advice from their pastors than the first ladies feeling he is more qualified. Hebrews 12:14 says follow peace with all men and holiness without which no man can see the Lord. In Genesis 50:20, Joseph told his brothers they meant evil against him, but God turned it around for good. No matter who comes against you, if you continue to love and pray for them, God will see you through.

Jeremiah 29:12 says we can call upon God, and He will hear us. However, we should be able to lean on trustworthy members of the body of Christ in our times of need. There should be no division in the body. We should be genuinely concerned about each other. If one part suffers, every part suffers with it; if one part is honored, every part rejoices with it. You are the body of Christ, and each one of us is a part of it (1 Corinthians 12:12).

Chapter 10

NAVIGATING CHURCH POLITICS

When the pastor and his wife unite as one, God is in the midst of them (Matthew 18:20). We must be more determined than that lowdown nothing of an Enemy. We must continue to "Fight the good fight of faith; lay hold on eternal life whereunto thou art also called and hast professed a good profession before many witnesses" (1 Timothy 6:12). Beware! That foul spirit Leviathan will try to come between you and your husband. As soon as you and your husband are each other's ride and die, he will come against you by using people you esteem highly.

A church member got angry with me for changing the order of the program. As a result, she left the church taking three young members with her. Of course, I felt bad about the situation, as did my husband. However, my husband announced to the church that as the first lady, I have the right to change the program as I am led to. Perhaps the member should have looked at our church program because it serves as a reminder to the saints, "This program is subject to change without notice." Although we were disappointed when they left, it brought me comfort to know that my husband publicly had my back. It's a shame three young people stopped attending church completely because of something so trivial.

I remember a time my husband and I attended our district meeting. The first three nights were wonderful; the Spirit of the Lord was present, and the anointing of the Holy Ghost was flowing. On the fourth night, which was the night I was in charge of the women's service, I felt a shift in the service. All of the pastors' wives who attended each night were pleasant; we all knew our places and the order of service. As the chairperson of the women's department for the district, my orders came directly from our district missionary.

The Spirit of Confusion

As service was going on, I looked around not knowing what was off and realized our superintendent's wife had just walked in. In fact, she had not been to the services for the first three nights. About eight of us first ladies were sitting in a particular section for all three nights. Yet, on this night, an usher was instructed by the superintendent's wife to move me around from one seat to another. I had to tell the usher I came to have church, not to play musical chairs.

When the superintendent's wife showed up that night, she did not come alone. She brought another spirit with her: the spirit of confusion. The entire atmosphere changed, but I prayed through it.

I felt a shift in the service.

The next night, my husband was in charge of the teaching session. Everyone there was engaged and understood the lesson, and the Spirit of the Lord was flowing. Abruptly, everyone suddenly became quiet. The superintendent's wife from the night before stood up. She made an absurd statement that created an atmosphere of confusion, causing several people to leave. That Enemy thought he was going to destroy the service; however, what the Enemy thought he could use against my husband's teaching, God meant it for good (Genesis 50:20).

My husband and I have been told by close Christian friends, church acquaintances, and even leaders within our organization that God said they are to bless us and put us in prestigious positions in the church. What amazing revelations.

Unfortunately, they never followed through. Since then, God has called a few of them to glory. I must admit that it was a very uncomfortable experience, but we never stopped loving them. We did not let their behavior affect our attendance or our financial support. We know the Enemy comes to steal, kill, and destroy, but we also know if God is for us who can be against us (Romans 8:31). We can't be stopped, and we won't be stopped because we are more than conquerors (Romans 8:37).

If God is for us who can be against us.

Church Folks

Stay focused, especially when it comes to dealing with members of your church. God created all people, but everyone attending church does not come to serve Him. There are several types of people who attend church:

God's members – These are the saints who are saved, sanctified, and filled with the Holy Ghost. These members love God with all of their hearts, minds, and souls. They love everyone. They don't give the pastor, his wife, or the church any problems. Their purpose is to win souls and help build the body of Christ.

Pastor's members – These are the people who attend church solely for the pastor. They only come when they are certain he will be there. These members only want the pastor to preach. He is the only one who can lay hands on them during prayer. He is the only one who can speak into their lives and instruct them. They are not concerned about giving offerings to anyone else but the pastor. These members always give the pastor birthday gifts, Christmas gifts, and take him out to dinner. They will even fix food for the pastor. They will call the pastor and wife's home and ask to speak to the pastor without acknowledging his wife. James 2:9 says to show favoritism is a sin.

Church's members – These people attend the church out of respect because they feel condemned if they don't. Most often they have grown up attending church. They do not want to join any of the auxiliaries in the church; they are comfortable just being Sunday morning saints.

The "want to be seen" members – These members come to church for one reason only... to be seen! They prance around the church so you can see their latest attire or new hairstyle. They will do anything to be seen even if it means disrupting the house of God.

The first lady's members – These are usually very few in number. They are the few who cater to the first lady's needs and protect her. They are not interested in anyone else joining their small circle. Though the support may feel nice, first ladies must be careful that the members close to her do not form a clique, drive others away, or make others feel unwelcomed.

Satan's members – These are the ones who come to sit in their special seats and if anyone dares sit in them, they are ready to fight. They criticize everything that goes on in the church. They can't ever say anything pleasant because there is nothing good in them. They are troublemakers and liars who are there to cause confusion. Whenever they are in your presence, they bring a foul spirit with them. They simply come to steal, kill, and destroy (John 10:10).

Praise and worship members – These are the ones who come to church for the free concert. They will be on time for service to get their seats and secure a mic, but don't look for them to be in Sunday school, Bible study, or prayer. When the music stops, they check out.

Ushers – These members have the reputation of being some of the meanest people in the church. Beware of those white gloves! The look on their faces will tell you not to ask them to do their job. Bring your own envelopes with you and think twice before you ask for a fan or a program. Not every usher is this way. Can we say thank God for the greeters? Galatians 6:10 reminds us to do good unto all men, especially those in the household of faith.

411 members – These are members who prey on the new visitors and members. Their sole purpose is to try and find out what type of sin you have committed so they can categorize you and spread your business. They are not looking for friends or to lead you to God. They just want to keep tabs on you.

God's Blueprint

Division is not God's design for His church. God has chosen us as leaders to oversee His church. He has given us a direct blueprint on how it is to be designed and carried out. However, pastors and first ladies have sat back for years and allowed our churches to become disorganized. We have accepted the wrong design for so long that if we try to do it God's way, chances are the only members left standing in the church would be the pastors, first ladies, and their families. If we don't stand up for what's right, we will inevitably fall for wrong. The church should be joined together in the same mind.

> Now I plead with you, brethren, by the name of our Lord Jesus Christ, that you all speak the same thing, and *that* there be no divisions among you, but *that* you be perfectly joined together in the same mind and in the same judgment. (1 Corinthians 1:10 NKJV)

First ladies have the power to redesign the church to the original plan of God. The key is to stay focused on God and use the gifts He has placed within us. When we do this, the churches will begin to grow with grace and compassion. The anointing will once again flow, and we won't feel constrained.

Thank God they are even attending the house of God.

Though the church consists of different types of members, some for the wrong reasons, we must thank God they are even attending the house of God. They are not allowing the Enemy to give them excuses to be absent. This is where your gifts come into play. You should let your light so shine before men that they can see your good works and glorify our Father in heaven (Matthew 5:16).

Matthew 13:30 says let the wheat and tares grow together. The house of God is a place for everyone to attend and seek help from God. Unfortunately, everyone is not coming to receive help from Him. It is the same way that Judas was with Jesus. Jesus knew that Judas was not going to change his traitorous ways. Yet, Jesus let him remain among Him and the other disciples. God came to this world to save all souls. If people with issues continue to come to church and never get delivered, this is because they have a love affair with their condition that is stronger than their relationship with God.

Every first lady and pastor would like everyone to leave the church delivered from the problems that they came with. If you have a condition, would you continue seeing the same doctor if they couldn't give you any medication that could help you?

Again, I encourage you to stay focused on God and what He has placed inside of you. You are so much more than how you feel. When you are faced with uncomfortable circumstances, know you have the power to turn them around. Look for the good in everything; combat darkness with your light.

It is okay to let someone else help you even if it concerns those nearest to your heart like your children and grandchildren. My husband and I experienced this often with our daughters. Sometimes when my husband gives them instructions or advice, they do not understand him. However, when I talk with them on the same matter, they understand. This hurts my husband's ego, but he will get over it.

I had to deal with one of our deacons in the church who would never join my prayer line. He would always get into the pastor's line and let him pray for him but not me. It used to make me feel bad but eventually, I got over it. Now, I am just happy he is getting into the line to receive prayer.

Let me reiterate a previous point: just because we are first ladies, it doesn't mean everyone will receive us with open arms. It also doesn't mean we have done anything wrong or that we are not anointed. It could mean people are rightfully exercising their freedom of choice. Do not let the Enemy tell you anything different.

It Takes a Village

When God places someone in your children or grandchildren's lives who can help them, let them. When you have tried or you know you are out of your lane concerning their needs, open up to someone who can help. Please step back and let someone who is willing and knowledgeable in the area of their need deal with the situation. This might be hard to handle but believe me when I say that sometimes other people can work better in certain areas of our children's lives than we or our husbands can.

Sometimes your child may understand another person better than you. This is not taking anything from you or your husband; it is not an insult to your parenting skills. You just want your children to do what is right and to get it right, so there is no room for jealousy, envy, or strife. It really does take a village to help raise our children. This is really what our lives in Christ are all about–to reach all. What a wonderful reason why God created us to be first ladies.

Chapter 11

HOW TO OWN YOUR DAY

First ladies, don't let anyone or anything put you in a box or make you feel that Sundays are the only days you can own your day. Don't let anyone or anything make you feel that Women's Day or the 5th Sundays are the only times you can own your day. Don't let anyone or anything make you feel your birthday or Mother's Day are the only days you can own your day. The Devil is a liar. Every day is the day that the Lord has made and as first ladies, we will rejoice and be glad in it (Psalm 118:24). Own it!

Since God loves me enough to bless me to see another day, I am going to speak how my day will be. I own my day by speaking prosperity over my life and the lives of my family members (Proverbs 18:21). When sickness tries to visit my body, I own my day by telling it that Jesus was wounded for my transgressions. He was bruised for my iniquities. The chastisement of my peace was upon Him, and by His stripes I am healed (Isaiah 53:5). When trouble sneaks up on me, I own my day by letting trouble know God is my refuge and strength, a very present help in trouble (Psalm 46:1). When the Enemy tries to make me feel like everyone is against me, I own my day by reminding him that greater is God in me, then the Enemy in the world (1 John 4:4).

First ladies, I want to personally let you know that you are fearfully and wonderfully made (Psalm 139:14). You don't ever have to feel left out from receiving your blessings.

> For the Lord God is a sun and shield; the Lord bestows favor and honor; no good thing does he withhold from those whose walk is blameless. (Psalm 84:11)

You are in control of your life. You are responsible for how your day, week, month, and year will turn out. According to the apostle Paul...

> We are troubled on every side, yet not distressed; we are perplexed, but not in despair; Persecuted, but not forsaken; cast down, but not destroyed.
> (2 Corinthians 4:8- 9)

Still, with all of these things going on in our lives, God has our back. He has assured us that He will never leave us or forsake us. He will be with us always, even until the end of the world (Matthew 18:20; Hebrews 13:5).

When you wake up in the morning, put on one of your husband's shirts or his pair of socks. Fix your favorite drink or snack. Play your favorite song. Watch a TV show or grab your favorite book. Sit down in your favorite chair. Enjoy life!

You are in control of your life.

You have been chosen by God to help your husband build the kingdom of God by using your God-given gifts. This is an honor. We have great work to do in this ministry. We will not give up, rust out, or faint. We will work until God says, "Well done thou good and faithful servant," until we can say without a shadow of a doubt, we have fought a good fight. We have finished the course and have kept the faith (Matthew 25:21; 2 Timothy 4:7).

The Meaning of First Ladies

F - first on the battlefield fighting for our God and Savior

I - inspired to win

R - resist every Devil that comes our way

S - serious about serving God

T - trusting God with every step we make

L - live to love

A - always praise our God

D - driven by passion

I - independent women who think for themselves

E - God's grace is everlasting

S - our souls are anchored in the Lord

Chapter 12

INTIMACY AND THE FIRST LADY

Intimacy is the close familiarity or friendship between a husband and wife. People often confuse it with sex, but you can be sexual without being intimate. Broadly speaking, intimacy means deeply knowing another person and in turn, feeling deeply known. This can happen during a conversation or in a coffee shop. It may occur on a lovely day at the beach or even at times during sex.

Maybe you are wondering why I am talking about intimacy in a Christian book. Well, intimacy is very important. As a matter of fact, if our parents were not intimate with each other, we would not be here (Genesis 2:24-25).

Believe it or not, men and women define intimacy a bit differently. For men, the development of intimacy can often be more physical than women. This is because men are physical creatures by nature. At times, it may seem more difficult for men to be intimate beyond the physical realm, but that doesn't mean they don't need or want it. On the other hand, women feel intimacy through emotional connection. For us, intimacy blossoms more when we engage in conversation than in sex itself. Even if a woman has an orgasm, sex is not completely satisfying without the close feelings that come with intimacy. Nonetheless, intimacy is something all humans crave.

There are four types of intimacy I want to share with you:

- ♥ Experimental intimacy: when people bond doing leisure activities
- ♥ Emotional intimacy: when people feel safe sharing their deepest feelings with each other
- ♥ Intellectual intimacy: when people feel comfortable sharing ideas and opinions even when they disagree
- ♥ Spiritual intimacy: when you and your spouse feel a close connection with God at the same time for the same purpose

It is important that I talk to Christians, especially husbands and wives about intimacy. For so long we have always considered intimacy to be a dirty word. It is a hush word, a word that we keep inside of us, and we only speak about it when we are in the comfort of our own homes. That's not the way it ought to be.

Intimacy will make you happier in your marriage. It makes it difficult for the Enemy to come into your marital life and cause problems as he often does. 1 Corinthians 7:1-40 says husbands should give conjugal rights to their wives and likewise, the wives to their husbands. Neither husbands nor wives have authority over their own bodies. The husband has authority over his wife's body and the wife has authority over her husband's body. You should not deprive each other of sexual pleasure except by mutual agreement. This should be for a short time to devote yourselves to fasting and prayer. However, you should resume sexual relations before Satan tempts you to sin because of your lack of self-control (1 Corinthians 7:5).

Intimacy will make you happier in your marriage.

Many times, we misunderstand this passage of Scripture. The Bible is not saying you must always say yes to sex with your husband or vice versa. Sometimes there is so much going on: children, work, ministry, etc. We get tired; sometimes we are not always in the mood for sex or intimacy. That does not mean we are sinning, or that something is wrong with us. Yes, Scripture does say our bodies belong to our husbands and vice versa but at the same time, we must have compassion for each other.

Husbands must be understanding and considerate. When their wives say they are tired or need a moment, they ought not to pout and get upset. First ladies must be equally understanding and considerate. Do not take no as rejection; it has nothing to do with you personally. It does, however, have everything to do with us clearing our minds and centering our thoughts on how wonderful it will be once we come back together. We could be thinking of some new moves that we have been inspired to share with each other. Don't let your relationship turn bland; nothing is wrong with adding a little spice to your marriage.

Ladies, we must also acknowledge our husbands have so much more on their plates than we can ever imagine. They have lots of responsibilities: dealing with the local, district, state, and national church. I will not even mention the personal matters that weigh on them in their quest to give us comfortable lifestyles. It may be a blessing they do not share everything with us.

> Trust in the LORD and do good; dwell in the land and enjoy safe pasture. Delight yourself in the LORD and he will give you the desires of your heart. Commit your way to the LORD; trust in him and he will do this: He will make your righteousness shine like the dawn, the justice of your cause like the noonday sun.
> (Psalm 37:3-6)

Take Time Out for Yourself

It is important for us to take care of our health and get rest. Our bodies will always let us know when it's time to rest and have physical check-ups. Whatever you do, don't ignore the signs. First ladies are always on the go doing things for our husbands, children, the church, and other family members. It is possible for us to forget to take time out for ourselves.

It is okay to take a day for yourself.

I have always said, in order to shop well for someone else you have to first be a great shopper for yourself. In other words, to take care of someone else, we must take care of ourselves first. This means it is okay to take a day for yourself.

Take time out to shop for yourself. Get your hair and nails done. Get a pedicure, waxing, and massage. You need it and you deserve it. Also, don't forget to stay physically active. Your body will always let you know when it's time for you to do some exercise. Everyone doesn't go to the gym, and you might not have a daily exercise routine but do something to stay in shape. You owe it to yourself.

> Beloved I wish above all that you prosper in health even as your soul prospereth. (3 John 1:2)

It is great to have a lot of money and the finer things in life, but you need good health to go along with that. The last thing you want is to be confined to your bed unable to help yourself. You do not want your husband or a nurse to have to take care of you. I mean, life happens, and it is possible that no matter what you do, you may get sick. However, you are responsible for living your best life.

> What? know ye not that your body is the temple of the Holy Ghost which is in you, which ye have of God, and ye are not your own?
>
> (1 Corinthians 6:19)

Every day you wake up say, "I feel good! I will do some type of exercise even if it's just walking." Then, make it happen. Make your day what you want it to be. Do you want to leave all of your wonderful blessings God has given you and your husband for another woman to come in and take? I know it might sound selfish to you, but you'll get over it.

God has blessed you and your spouse, so it's time for you to start enjoying your blessings. You can do this by watching what you eat and taking care of your health. We must also see to it that our husbands are eating right and exercising. I know they can be stubborn and give us problems. Some of our husbands may say they don't need us to worry about their weight; they can do it themselves; and that's fine. Let them watch it, but you watch it too.

Take Care of Each Other

Your husband belongs to you just as much as you belong to your husband. You said in your vows that you would stay together in health and in sickness until death do you part, so why not live a wonderful, prosperous life together? This is what God planned for you.

Do you know Christians have a higher divorce rate than non-Christians? That's a serious dilemma. Does it have anything to do with a lack of intimacy in the marriage? Perhaps. As I said before, intimacy is very important when it comes to husbands and wives. As a matter of fact, as far as I am concerned, intimacy is more important than sex. Now, I know you may disagree with me and say I must not be doing it right. Well, this is a subjective matter, so I'll let you be the judge.

Intimacy between a husband and wife creates a private, cozy atmosphere, a sense of peace. Sometimes you may feel like sitting close together, holding each

other's hands, hugging, laying on each other's chest or laps. That's intimacy. When you find yourselves simply talking, laughing, and reminiscing about pleasant experiences you shared years ago and the ones you look forward to–that's intimacy.

Frankly, sometimes sex happens so quickly you don't even enjoy or remember it. Now, I'm not trying to hurt anyone's feelings. I'm merely saying it's totally different from being intimate. Intimacy lasts much longer and sometimes it's all you need. I won't dare try to tell you what works and doesn't work in your marriage; I will leave that conversation up to you and your spouse. What I know to be true is that intimacy can lead to sex. The more intimacy you share the more and better sex you will have. I'm just saying give it a try.

Intimacy Is Always

The good thing about intimacy is that you can have it whether you are elderly, ill, injured, impotent, or otherwise incapacitated. If sex is the highlight of your marriage, you will be in for a big surprise if you are ever faced with some of these challenges.

Intimacy takes the place of sex to some extent. You can show affection, cuddle up with each other, blow in each other's ears, and kiss each other's hands. You can talk about when you first met. Reminisce on the days you took your vows as you looked into each other's eyeballs and pledged to stay together in sickness and in health.

The time may come when your spouse is unable to please you sexually. You must take care of each other. You cannot put your spouse away; you must be patient, caring, and loving. This is why it's so important to take care of each other's health and not be selfish. Do not say you will take

care of your body and whatever your husband does with his is up to him. No! You take care of your body and you try to help your husband take care of his. It works both ways.

As mentioned earlier, 1 Corinthians Chapter 7 is an important part of Scripture for husbands and wives. Verse 4 says the wife has no power over her own body but the husband. Likewise, the husband has no power over his own body but the wife. This is to ensure that the woman gets the sexual satisfaction she deserves and the husband does too. That way, everyone is happy.

I tell ladies to take care of themselves. Always look good and smell good, even when you are at home. Some women think because they are working at home with the children and taking care of the house they have an excuse for being unkempt. But believe it or not; it's a turn-off. Your husband does not want to come home to an untidy wife.

I make sure if I don't have my hair styled, the scarf on my head matches whatever I am wearing. I use perfume every day, all day. My lips always have something on them, even if they're just shining. I wear my earrings also. This may be extreme for some of you; however, you should always look presentable and smell good because you are still the first lady.

It's so important to take care of each other's health.

You should be the first sweet-smelling person your husband encounters in the morning. You should be the first lady your husband smells when he comes home. Leave the smell of your sweet perfume on him all day long. It's a blessing for him. As your fragrance lingers on him so will his thoughts of you. He will long to return home for the smell and what will come along with it.

Openly Display Affection

As I said earlier, I never saw my parents showing affection to each other. I discussed this with my older sisters and brothers, and they confirmed this. This lack of affection was passed down to us as children. As a result, my husband calls my family the "touch me not family." This is how it appears until you get to know us. We actually love each other very much. As a matter of fact, we are very tight as a family; we just display our love differently compared to other families.

As your fragrance lingers so will his thoughts of you.

Growing up we didn't hug each other or say I love you, but we knew we loved one another; nothing could come between us. We only started telling each other I love you after our mother passed away. We actually spoke the words and are now getting more and more comfortable saying it. If God asked me what type of family I would like, I would say to God, "Give me the exact family you have already given me." The only thing I would want God to do for my family is to make us more affectionate and to save, sanctify, and fill with the Holy Ghost those who are not.

Unfortunately, my husband never saw his mother or father being affectionate toward each other either. His father would always show affection to all of his children. However, anytime his father tried to display similar affection to his mother, it was not received well. She would simply move away from him. He never saw his parents holding hands, kissing, or hugging, even though they loved each other.

I don't know if this is specific to our family or if this is something that is common among many Christians. I have so many relatives who are pastors' kids and they all say the same thing: their parents were not affectionate. Now, don't get me wrong; there are pastors and first ladies who are very loving toward each other and their children and to that I say hats off to you.

I have been married for thirty-one years. The only thing I would change about being married would be to marry my husband sooner than I did. My mother always told us when we were young, one thing we must do before we leave this world is to experience marriage. She said we had to at least try it once because being married allows you to be 100% yourself at all times.

In marriage, you know you can always be yourself. You don't have to try to be someone you're not. You don't have to hide. You always have someone who will laugh with you. Now, you might have someone who doesn't laugh with or at you, but that's not your fault. Chances are he probably needs you to pinch his ear or slap him on his bottom.

Pastors and first ladies talk to people, laugh with them, and desire to know how they are doing. They hug them and hold their hands. However, when it comes to our own spouses, we seem to somehow forget. Learn how to show your spouse affection.

Keep Laughing

Six months after my husband and I were married, we were walking through the parking lot headed to one of our favorite stores. Before we entered the store, a nice-looking car with a lovely African American couple drove up. They stopped us and said, "Whatever you two are laughing about, be sure to keep laughing the same way after you have gotten married."

My husband and I looked at them and said in unison, "We are married."

They were in a rush but wished we could have given them our secret to being happily married. At the time, my husband and I were laughing at something that had happened to us just before we were married. Until this day, if we mention that conversation, we still burst out laughing the same way. By the way, the couple who stopped us served as the pastor and first lady at the church my two sisters were attending.

Now that I think about it, I am going to have to remind my husband about this more often than I do. If our laughter, holding hands, and joy caught this couples' attention, how much more attention can we get now? It's worth a try.

If you and your husband have problems showing affection, think about something so hilarious it has you holding hands and laughing out loud. People will wonder if you are dating. This statement still rings true: "If you don't cherish your spouse, you can lose your spouse." Maybe not for a long time, but I don't want to lose my husband at any time.

I must admit to you that I asked my husband way back in the day to teach me how to be affectionate. He tried, but I failed several times for many years. Now, when I ask him, he says, "No, if you have not learned by now, you will never learn. You're too old now." I still ask him, and we laugh about it.

> For with God, nothing shall be impossible. (Luke 1:37)

> Again, truly I tell you that if two of you on earth agree about anything they ask for, it will be done for them by my Father in heaven. (Matthew 18:19 NIV)

When God created man and woman, He looked at all He had done, and it was pleasing in His sight. God saw everything He made and behold it was very good (Genesis 1:31). When the scripture says "everything," it includes how He designed our bodies. I want you to clearly understand that God intended for us to enjoy sexual relations in the covenant of marriage. Sex was designed by God, not the world. He made it for procreation *and* pleasure. It is a time when you and your husband can express your love to one another.

Once again, I must mention the issue concerning our weight because it is such a huge part of why so many first ladies feel depressed. Sometimes you may gain or lose weight. At these times, the Enemy comes to make you feel badly about yourself or each other. You and your spouse must stop, have a seat, develop a plan and discuss how and when you will begin exercising together. You might start of walking, but before you know it, you will be jogging. Eventually, you will find yourself saying to one another, "The first one in the shower gets to decide how long you will stay in."

Our bodies are the temples of the Holy Ghost. Our bodies are not our own; they belong to God. Yes, He cares about what we eat. He created our bodies in such a way that we need certain nutrients to survive. Don't just do it because you know it's good for you or to get your doctor or spouse to stop hounding you. Don't do it for the Instagram picture to prove you can do it. Do it for God. Show how much you really appreciate Him for allowing you to have the will and faith to take care of what He has blessed you with.

Be Comfortable in Your Own Skin

Ladies, don't be insecure about your appearance. Genesis 1:27 reminds us that we are made in God's image. I have never allowed the Enemy to cause me to worry about anyone else taking my husband. First of all, if my husband is foolish enough to allow God to bless another man with me, then he truly needs more of Jesus.

Secondly, if any woman could take him, he was never mine. I own everything God has blessed me with every day. Every day is my day that the Lord has made for me. I refuse to be depressed. I will rejoice and be glad in it (Psalm 118:24).

Own your talents and God-given gifts. Own your bedroom. Own your intimacy. Own your sexual desire. Own being a first lady. OWN YOUR DAY!

ACKNOWLEDGMENTS

I will forever appreciate my husband of thirty-one years, Superintendent Ronald Omega Blake and my three daughters, Rachel, Ron-esha, and Rae-Ocean Blake. Thank you for your endless encouragement as I wrote this book.

I truly believe in my heart that being a first lady is a position ordained by God. It is not made by men or women. It is a position that comes from deep within a woman's soul, spirit, and heart. It is a connection God put in a woman just as the connection He places in a mother. It is an internal root He has planted in a woman deep within.

Being a first lady is a love, a feeling of compassion and concern for others no one else has the patience for. It is the longing that makes her want to help empower other women in whom God has placed a desire to help build His kingdom. It is the love and enduring strength from God that makes the first lady push her husband and family to the greatness God has already placed within them.

Special thank you to Ron-esha as she was instrumental in bringing this book fruition. Her tireless efforts, engaging in several rounds of editing to ensure this book was polished to perfection, but retained my authentic voice, are well deserving of mention.

CONGRATULATORY NOTES

To my beloved, you have given me 31 years of matrimonial bliss and never a dull moment. You've given me three beautiful and intelligent daughters, two pursuing careers as medical doctors and one as a scientist. God called you at a very young age and you couldn't quite figure out why you couldn't go to the same excesses as your peers. Upon surrendering to the divine will of God, you henceforth ran for your life, teaching the gospel wherever God opened the door. You quite often operate in the gifts of word of wisdom and prophecy which is a blessing to the church. He has so wonderfully gifted you with an uncanny sense of beauty and fashion, which you display so effortless and fluidly–second to none (in my opinion). I can say for a surety that you possess the ability to make most women beautiful in appearance. God promoted you from being a deaconess to an evangelist, from a missionary to a district missionary and then to being the First Lady of Prayer Memorial Church of God in Christ. You are a devoted wife, mom, excellent role model to the women's department, prayer warrior, lover of God and His people. You are District Missionary Rachel D. Blake and you have my profound love.

–Superintendent
R. O. Blake

These are the things they don't tell you about being a First Lady! Expertly guiding you through it all, First Lady Blake leaves no stone unturned. She gives a contemporary insight into the realities of a high calling, serving alongside the pastor. Prepare to take out your notepad in this witty, yet lesson ridden book! Congratulations on your first of many books Mom! The journey has been well worth it!

–Rachel V. Blake

Mom, the way you poured yourself into this book daily no matter the circumstance is a testament to your commitment to do God's work. May it fill every vessel open to receive. You are such an inspiration!

–Ron-esha O. Blake

You kept adding more and more to this book. I started to wonder if you were not already a writer.
Your creativity is one of your best attributes.
Your inspiration with this book will surely
flow into many others you are sure to write.
Congrats on your first book Mom!

–Rae-Ocean A. Blake

ABOUT THE AUTHOR

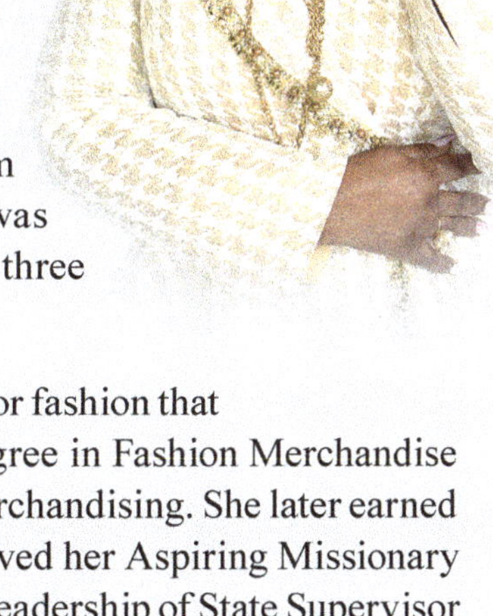

Lady Rachel Denise Blake was born in Bakersfield, CA to the late District Superintendent Norris Howard. Her mother was the late District Missionary Lucille Howard. Lady Blake is the seventh of eight children: four boys and four girls.

In November 1989, she and her husband were blessed to be married. After two years of their marriage, God answered their prayers by relocating them from Bakersfield to Denver, Colorado. He was also graceful enough to bless them with three beautiful daughters.

Lady Blake was gifted with such a love for fashion that she earned a Specialized Associates degree in Fashion Merchandise from the Scranton School of Fashion Merchandising. She later earned a second Associates in Travel. She received her Aspiring Missionary License in September of 1992 under the leadership of State Supervisor Perry Dean of the Northwest jurisdiction in Northern California.

Lady Blake also received her Evangelist Missionary License in 1997 under the leadership of Mother L. O. Wells in Denver. Her husband became a pastor in 2008. In 2012, she became a District Missionary of the Jireh District and a member of the RIJ Department of Women's Executive Board.

Lady Blake is currently an adult Sunday School teacher for the Prayer Memorial Church of God in Christ and the Women's Department Coordinator. As an intercessor, Lady Blake instituted the once-a-month prayer shut-in. She also has a great love for young people, which encouraged her to create the Youth Stepping Team.

She and her husband also hosted weekly youth meetings so that young people can fellowship and feel free to discuss whatever was on their minds. Lady Blake is also a strong advocate for the elderly.

Her ultimate goal is for everyone in this world to have their own mansion in heaven where hers will be pink with gold trimming. We end with her favorite scriptures:

> And, lo, I am with you always, even unto the end of the world. Amen.
>
> (Matthew 28:20 NKJV)

> I will never leave you nor forsake you.
>
> (Hebrews 13:5b NKJV)

> I have fought a good fight, I have finished my course, I have kept the faith. (2 Timothy 4:7-8)

ABOUT THE AUTHOR

Lady Rachel Denise Blake was born in Bakersfield, CA to the late District Superintendent Norris Howard. Her mother was the late District Missionary Lucille Howard. Lady Blake is the seventh of eight children: four boys and four girls.

In November 1989, she and her husband were blessed to be married. After two years of their marriage, God answered their prayers by relocating them from Bakersfield to Denver, Colorado. He was also graceful enough to bless them with three beautiful daughters.

Lady Blake was gifted with such a love for fashion that she earned a Specialized Associates degree in Fashion Merchandise from the Scranton School of Fashion Merchandising. She later earned a second Associates in Travel. She received her Aspiring Missionary License in September of 1992 under the leadership of State Supervisor Perry Dean of the Northwest jurisdiction in Northern California.

Lady Blake also received her Evangelist Missionary License in 1997 under the leadership of Mother L. O. Wells in Denver. Her husband became a pastor in 2008. In 2012, she became a District Missionary of the Jireh District and a member of the RIJ Department of Women's Executive Board.

Lady Blake is currently an adult Sunday School teacher for the Prayer Memorial Church of God in Christ and the Women's Department Coordinator. As an intercessor, Lady Blake instituted the once-a-month prayer shut-in. She also has a great love for young people, which encouraged her to create the Youth Stepping Team.

She and her husband also hosted weekly youth meetings so that young people can fellowship and feel free to discuss whatever was on their minds. Lady Blake is also a strong advocate for the elderly.

Her ultimate goal is for everyone in this world to have their own mansion in heaven where hers will be pink with gold trimming. We end with her favorite scriptures:

> And, lo, I am with you always, even unto the end of the world. Amen.
>
> (Matthew 28:20 NKJV)

> I will never leave you nor forsake you.
>
> (Hebrews 13:5b NKJV)

> I have fought a good fight, I have finished my course, I have kept the faith. (2 Timothy 4:7-8)

www.ingramcontent.com/pod-product-compliance
Lightning Source LLC
LaVergne TN
LVHW052347100826
845147LV00012B/770